THE BRIDGE

Sam Song

Trafford
PUBLISHING™

Order this book online at www.trafford.com/06-2872
or email orders@trafford.com

Most Trafford titles are also available at major online book retailers.

Note for Librarians: A cataloguing record for this book is available from Library
and Archives Canada at www.collectionscanada.ca/amicus/index-e.html

ISBN: 978-1-4251-1113-7

*We at Trafford believe that it is the responsibility of us all, as both individuals
and corporations, to make choices that are environmentally and socially sound.
You, in turn, are supporting this responsible conduct each time you purchase a
Trafford book, or make use of our publishing services. To find out how you are
helping, please visit www.trafford.com/responsiblepublishing.html*

*Our mission is to efficiently provide the world's finest, most comprehensive
book publishing service, enabling every author to experience success.
To find out how to publish your book, your way, and have it available
worldwide, visit us online at www.trafford.com/10510*

 www.trafford.com

North America & international
toll-free: 1 888 232 4444 (USA & Canada)
phone: 250 383 6864 ♦ fax: 250 383 6804 ♦ email: info@trafford.com

The United Kingdom & Europe
phone: +44 (0)1865 722 113 ♦ local rate: 0845 230 9601
facsimile: +44 (0)1865 722 868 ♦ email: info.uk@trafford.com

10 9 8 7 6 5 4 3 2

Table of Contents

Chapter3   Outsourcing

Chapte6   Case

Not the End

Appendix   1

Chinese Dynasties

Appendix   2

Thick Black School

Preface

China, regarded as "Middle Kingdom" and mysterious place, is a land of opportunity whilst a land of risk. When most western people deal with Chinese, they often feel confused or frustrated due to so many unknowns, so many variables, and so high uncertainty. Yes, I have the same feeling even I am a native Chinese. Why, different culture and business environment drive different human behaviors? I just want to share with my personal experience about life, career and marriage with you and give you some tips to improve your business prospect, to protect your personal privacy, to avoid conflict of "Office Politics" in China. Hence, you can get more insightful understanding about Chinese culture and business environment to reduce your risk and frustration and gain more profound idea and sound advice to get through it.

Born in China, I am not ashamed of it and have not lost hope even she has some daunting troubles and problems need to be solved or improved. But truth is truth. It will overcome smart human opinions and can be tested by time or history. China is a huge country, and her national life has too many facets. So, she does not require whitewashing. She will, as she always did, be right herself again as in *Tang Dynasty*.

This book is not "Travel guide", "Culture guide" or "Code of Management". It is about how to mitigate your business risk and how to live and work in China with practical key points. In this book I have tried to communicate my personal opinions with simple common sense, which I have reached after painful thought, unhappy experience, and introspection. And I will stand justified or condemned by this book. After you read it you will feel:

No Fear!

No Confusion!

No Frustration!

Chapter 1   Culture shock

People are good by nature

人之初，性本善

Lived more than 2,500 years ago, Confucius sorted out the books and records of the Xia and Shang dynasties with his disciples, created the philosophy of "benevolence", and taught people to exert moral instinct in their daily lives and behaviors, which involved politics, education, and ethics, and also the building of proper relationships among the people.

The structure of Confucian social philosophy was well-organized. Political system, administrative principles like policies of benevolence, light taxes, and ruling by rites were significant representative views in traditional Confucian thoughts. Therefore, it is Confucius who has shaped the ethics and outlooks of modern Chinese people. He is not so much a religion as it is a code for social conduct. However, his influence is so pervasive that people in China unconsciously function in a Confucian manner.

The critical part of Confucian philosophy is Rujiao (儒教) which has four essential qualities: Ren (benevolence), Yi (righteousness and loyalty), Dao (taking the right path), De (Virtue and morality). It is adopted by most of the Chinese emperors and rulers as a basis of government; the ethical code as propagated in the teaching of Rujiao is accepted as governing social conduct and public administration as well. The basic theme of this code is: obedience to and respect for superiors and parents, duty to family, loyalty to friends, humility, sincerity, and courtesy.

However, as social civilization development and technology advancement, young Chinese intellectuals are consciousness that China as she had been in the past was not able to meet the dangerous and aggressive modernity of the west. They argued: Confucian lived 2,500 years ago, how to know modern Chinese business would be like? In addition, he never taught his student how to run business, and no such word "management", "industry" or "competitive advantage" in his book. These young people have been battered by many forces of the new times and pushed for renewal and a departure from the undesirable aspects of traditional culture. They need modern political system, modern economy system, modern education system, modern science &technology system and modern military system. However, no matter you agree or not, Confucian manner is still a dominant Chinese culture today. Therefore, regarding modernization, the Confucian manner needs to be accommodated to fit modern development. Especially through Mao Zedong's ten years "Culture Revolution", Chinese behave more complex and have so many facets towards different circumstances. So, people just argue: human beings are good/evil by nature? Well, one of scholar of Confucian philosophy named Xunzi said: People are evil by nature （人之初，性本恶）.On the other hand, another scholar of Confucian philosophy named Liao said: People are good by nature, but evil by desire（人之初，性本善，但邪恶由欲望引起）

People are evil by nature 人之初，性本恶

1.11 Face and face reading

The tree needs peel, the people need face
树要皮，人要脸

The tree needs peel, the people need face （树要皮，人要脸）. Indeed, in Chinese business culture, a person's reputation and social standing rests on face. Causing embarrassment or loss of composure, even unintentionally, can be disastrous for business negotiation.

Face is how others view or judge of them as individuals or families. It is nothing to do with material benefits. Face can be demonstrated by person, group, corporation, even government. Therefore, sometimes saving face could result in a loss in view of the huge expenditure on the construction of oversized facilities.

Having face means having a high social status in the eyes of one's peers, and it is a mark of personal dignity and respect. So, Chinese are acutely sensitive to having and maintaining face in all aspects of social and business life. You should always be aware of the face factor when dealing with Chinese.

Keeping face is important for your business. However, face reading is another critical part to react or behave properly in your business deal. Face reading derives from Buddhist philosophy. The Chinese look at the face to see how the personality is built up according to five different elements. These are the Wood element, the Fire element, the Water element, the Metal element and the Earth element. The wood nourishes the fire and when the fire burns this creates the earth. The earth has a metal element in it and so the minerals and crystals within this when melted, creates the water.

Chinese doctors always use this deep knowledge of the personality and health of their patients by close observation of the face to aid diagnosis and treatment. Furthermore, face reading can also be used for building up a psychological and emotional profile which is a valuable tool in Human Resources and Career Planning especially in selecting CEO.

1.12 Guanxi (关系)

Guanxi is a central concept in Chinese society and describes, in part, a personal relationship or connection between two people in which one is able to prevail upon another to perform a favor or service, or be prevailed upon. In the Chinese business world, however, it is also understood as the network of relationships among various parties that cooperate together and support each other. In essence, this boils down to exchanging interests, which are expected to be done regularly and voluntarily. Therefore, to succeed in China, you must cultivate close personal ties with business associates to earn their respect and trust. Most foreigners have often failed to attempt to establish long-term business in China because they did not recognize that business relationships were also personal relationships.

If you do not have Guanxi, you do not have anything. Everything in China seems to be in scarcity, and to get things done, you need to know people. Any successful person in China will be a member of a closed network of relatives, friends, and friends of friends, classmates, and associates with shared interests. These people do favor for one another and always seek a rough balance between help given and received.

Therefore, getting the wide and right "Guanxi", the organization can minimize the risks, frustrations, and disappointments when doing business in China. Often it is acquiring the right "Guanxi" with the relevant authorities that will determine the competitive advantage of an organization in the long run in China. And moreover, the inevitable risks, barriers, and setbacks you'll encounter in

China will be minimized when you have the right "Guanxi" network working for you. That's the important of Guanxi and it has its roots in the traditional concept of family. For Chinese, individuals are parts of family whole. The family is the source of identity, protection, and bond. In term of hardship, war, or social chaos, the Chinese family structure was a basic against the brutal outside world, in which no one and nothing could be trusted. As a result, trust and cooperation were reserved for family members and extremely close friends. Moreover, China was and continues to be a land rules more by decree than laws. A high official could act with impunity, and innocent people could get hurt unless they had powerful friends to protect them.

Hence, the difficulty in cultivating solid relationship can be the biggest obstacle to succeed in China. So, be patient and try your best to build it.

1.13 Greed

There are two tragedies in life:

one is not getting what you want; the other is getting it.

The English wit Oscar Wilde said: "There are two tragedies in life: one is not getting what you want; the other is getting it." Exactly! It is common sense that you will feel upset when you can not get what you want. The real tragedy is even you get what you want you are still not satisfied. Because after you get something, you expect more. It is greed. According the definition of dictionary: Greed is an excessive desire to acquire or possess more than what one needs or deserves, especially with respect to material wealth. It can be exhibited by person, group, corporation, even government; and it is qualitative, immeasurable, and can not be judged by moral standard which is good or bad. Different personality shows different greed. Sometimes, simple greed does not require intention. However, most of time, greed is not impulsive, it is planned and calibrated.

If you use it to improve your quality service, it is a good thing for continuous improvement; on the other hand, it is an evil desire that drives you crazy. From definition of greed you see, the key point is 'more than need'. Indeed, people never satisfy themselves. To be a departmental manager, corporate CEO, no, it is not enough, even as a country's President, still not. One wishes to be a King of the world, still not enough. Everyone must obey to him, follow to him, and worship to him. So, greed—selfish—jealousness......it is endless game. Although we are bored and tired of it we are still struggle for it.

It is true for Chinese indeed, they expect more—more food, money, power, or possession; furthermore, the Chinese as opportunists are seldom satisfied with what they have on hand if the next person has more wealth or business. It is often greed that eventually leads to their downfall. In this regard, Chinese are truly inveterate gamblers as well. They haunt casinos and racecourses as well as stock exchanges. They never stop scouting around for opportunities. The moment a business proves successful, others will jump on to the bandwagon.

Only greed, people have wants and needs, out there potential opportunities and prospects for your business. From this point, it is not a bad thing.

1.14 The "Iron rice bowl" (铁饭碗)

"Iron rice bowl", in Chinese term, was lifelong guaranteed employment system, because China, as a country, is a huge well that never running dry after year 1949.

Therefore, all workers and farmers were put together under strictly state control. Especially for workers, their work units controlled every aspect of daily life, including the allocation of housing, food and clothing. The work units also decided who could marry and when, and who was allowed to have children. So, most factories were overmanned with more slackers. And, all got exactly the same pay and privileges. Each of them had a tiny flat that was virtually rent free, enjoyed the same subsidized food and got the same miserable pay—**"Big Pot Meal" (大锅饭)** phenomenon. Therefore, why should one person work while a dozen did as little as possible? It encouraged "average" and laziness, discouraged working harder, competition and innovation.

So, this build-in social ill that invariably resulted in low productivity, quality defects, delivery delays, breakdown of equipment due to lack of routine maintenance and factories missing deadline for orders. Moreover, the service attitude of government officers was unacceptable because they knew they could not be sacked.

Currently, China's Central Government has reformed it and abrogated lifelong employment system. However, the result is still not desirable in state-own companies and government agencies or institutions.

1.15 Nepotism

Yi ren de dao, ji quan shang tian 一人得道,鸡犬上天

If one succeeds, his chicken and dog will fly up to heaven too

"Yi ren de dao, ji quan shang tian", （一人得道，鸡犬上天）（if one succeeds, his chicken and dog will fly up to heaven too) that is Nepotism in Chinese term. Nepotism essentially means making a special effort or sacrifice to provide timely support to one's relatives and friends because to do the best for one's relatives or friends is fundamental Rujiao. It is a social obligation on the part of a high official or a wealthy person to maintain an open house for his needy relatives and friends. Therefore, if your relatives or friends have higher social status, everything will turn green for you. Moreover, Nepotism means Cronyism because only relatives and friends can be trusted and can bring security to them. Every family in China is really a communistic unit, with the principle of "do what you can and take what you need" guiding its functions. Mutual helpfulness is developed to a very high degree, encouraged by a sense of moral obligation and family honor. A successful man, if he is an official, always gives the best jobs to his relatives, and if there are not ready jobs, he can create ones.

A tendency towards Nepotism is instinctual, a form of kin selection. It is quite natural; therefore, that charity should begin at home. For the family system must be taken as the Chinese traditional system if insurance against unemployment.

1.16 Apolitical

In West, most people enjoy life, however, in China, most people struggle for life. Verily, in China, life for most Chinese has always been rough and tough through different ages. However, in their quest to accumulate wealth, Chinese do not seek political eminence with a view to serving the community. They are family—minded, not social-minded, and the family mind is only a form of magnified selfishness. Like playing game, most Chinese do not play team-work game; they would rather play most popular game "majong" as the essence of Chinese individualism.

Therefore, Chinese abstain from talking politics; they do not cast votes really or votes just as a form, and they have no clubhouse debates on politics. So, when there is trouble outside the house, they simply close the doors and wait it out just like proverb "Sweep the snow in front of his door, and do not bother about the frost on his neighbor's roof". （各人自扫门前雪，不管他人瓦上霜）When there is a serious accident, the others cars simply drive past as it is perceived to be the job of the police and the ambulance. It does not mater to them whether help will arrive timely because it is none business of them.

**Sweep the snow in front of his door,
and do not bother about the frost on his neighbor's roof**

各人自扫门前雪，不管他人瓦上霜

1.17 Filial Piety

In Confucian and Buddhist thought, filial piety, Chinese termed **"Xiao Shun"** （孝顺） is considered the first virtue in Chinese culture: a love and respect to one's parents and ancestors. Therefore, all the parents and the elderly received good care from their children in their old ages are taken in Chinese tradition as proof of a good society and a good government. So, to build an ideal society, the family relationship is an essential part. Family is the cell of the society, and archons of past dynasties all paid great attention to the stability of families, which affected the stability of the society and the regime of the archon as well. Exactly, not having children to carry on the family name amounts to breaking the ancestral linkage, it is regard as the most serious filial failure. So, the bigger family, the stronger it is. However, sons get the family fortune and daughters none, unless there are no male theirs. And the biggest share goes to the eldest son. Parents have to depend on their children in their old age. They are confident their sons will not abandon them because it is their obligation of taking good care of their aged parents.

Therefore every family needs at least one son especially in countryside. However due to modern Chinese government strictly "Birth Control" policy (City has one, countryside permits two) some families can not get the son because of limitation. To avoid heavy penalty for over-born, they run away from home and try to born at least one son and dare not to register in Residential Committee. That's why so many children do not have household or resident permit and cannot receive proper education.

1.18 Inferiority complex

An inferiority complex is a feeling that one is inferior to others in some way. It is often unconscious, and is thought to drive afflicted individuals to overcompensate, resulting either in spectacular accomplishment or extreme antisocial behavior. Indeed, Chinese are socially sensitive. They like crowd and live in communities. Outside the home, they prefer to travel in groups to hide their vulnerability.

The inferiority complex, this vicious circle is common in neurotic lifestyles. The poorer or less educated a person, the more he perceives that others are looking down on him. To cover up his inferiority, he tends to speak loudly as though he is a person in substance. Or he may make an ill-afforded purchase really comes from the fondness of the Chinese to look down on others. It is not just the rich looking down on the poor. The poor looks down on the poor as well. Therefore, it was not surprising that some reports from EU or Japan that local people got shocked by Chinese crazy shopping in their tour group. Another related behavior is habitually showing off. This is especially so among those who are not really well known, wealthy or well educated. They take big and act big, well above their real status, just in case others do not happen to know their little success in life.

It is deemed intentionally offensive for a wealthier person to ridicule his friends or relatives because they do not buy a new car or send their children for overseas education, when he knows full well that they cannot afford it.

1.19 "Me–my–mine" syndromes

With typical family-minded of Chinese, the Chinese are a nation of individualists. That's why the Chinese are often rude or uncaring strangers when they deal with.

Therefore, Chinese individual draws a clear line what belongs to me, my family, my network, or my interest clique, and the rest of the other community; me, being the center of the world, to be followed by my immediate family members; my relatives distinguished by degrees of how close or distant their relationship; and those from the same village or town. I choose to be oblivious to the important of things or issues outside my personal network or world. It is what constitutes "Me–my–mine" or selfish in Chinese term.

This social ill confronts the Chinese as a society and a nation. As a result, National parts or reserves, expressways, temples and museums, and all other public places are not considered a part of the personal domain of any individual Chinese; moreover, we does not consider it our responsibility to keep public places tidy and clean. The offending person is simply not aware that his thoughtlessness and recklessness is causing serious environmental pollution that will affect him eventually. Indeed, it has become a filthy habit for drivers and passengers of vehicles in China to throw all kinds of garbage onto the road as a common public behavior.

1.20 Beings, ghosts and immortals

The Chinese are pragmatic and inclining to be materialistic, yet careful in their approach to the unknown. They accept birth and death as pre-ordained. What happen in between is largely a matter of self-determination, subject to the possible interference of ghosts and immortals.

Religion for most ordinary Chinese is essential and avenue for obtaining spiritual support to enhance their mortal livelihood. That's why so many Chinese mythical stories, either that created by the primitive people or those written by later scholars, are full of human feelings. Gods, ghosts, foxes and spirits are commonly described as living things with human qualities and human feelings. Chinese inventors of myths describe gods the way they describe man, or treat them as if they were human, and endow them with human nature.

And these mythical stories also try to illustrate fatalism, reincarnation, and all sorts of feudal ethical principles. This is only natural, because literary works inevitably reflect the beliefs of the age in which they are produced.

1.21 Culture of dining and drinking

Most people eat to live. However, Chinese live to eat. This is not an exaggeration but a simple fact of life. All Chinese, ancient or modern, rich or poor, adores food. That's why a polite traditional greeting is not "How are you?" but "Have you eaten?"

Dining, accompanying by tea or alcohol, is not only food, is considered as a culture.

1.211 Dining

Having been developed and refined by a unique culture over a period of more than five thousand years, Chinese cuisine is more than just basic nourishment. It is meant to feast the eyes, to please the palate, to "repose benignly on the stomach", and to ensure optimum health. Therefore, emperors, poets and warriors were expected to be connoisseurs of fine dining through the ages.

However, eating is not only for the above, but also for building relationship especially for social and business. Evening banquets are the most popular occasions for business entertaining. Therefore, waiting to be seated, as there is a seating etiquette based on hierarchy in Chinese business culture. Generally, the seat in the middle of the table, facing the door, is reserved for the host. The most senior guest of honor sits directly to the left. Everyone else is seated in descending order of status. The most senior member sits in the center seat. Follow this seating pattern if you are hosting a banquet or a meal in your residence, whether for business or purely social reasons. The host is the first person at the table allowed to begin eating by suggesting the first drink. Then, the rest of the company can proceed with the meal.

After banquet, a hardly Chinese host may invite you to go singing in karaoke club. For Chinese, the karaoke phenomenon is the most popular business and social entertainment of their natural prosperity to sing with close friends. If you wish to establish close relationship with Chinese, going to karaoke is one of the best ways of doing it.

1.212 Alcohol drinking

Alcohol drinking is not only one of the most common social activities in China, it has become so much a part of the culture it is practically impossible for someone to be Chinese if they do not indulge in social drinking. Therefore, every drinking occasion is an opportunity to improve relationship, gain respect and trust in China.

Forming a good personal relationship in your business dealing is very important. Part of this involves participating in the strong drinking culture that exists there. In general, Chinese regard with suspicion anyone who does not participate in the inevitable drinking that takes place during almost all business dinners. And it is at these kinds of social occasions that most negotiating breakthroughs are made.

Hence all those attending dinner have to do their fair share of drinking. Every drinker is also expected to force others to drink their fair as well. Every drinker must offer at least one toast (most three toasts) to every attendance at every business or social dinner. Apart from the normal practice of encouraging others to drink, the Chinese have devised a simple finger-guessing game to make it easier to encourage others to drink more and more. Therefore, drinking alcohol is a skill the Chinese have been honing for several thousand years, so visiting businesspeople are strongly advised not to try to out-drink them or even match them glass for glass.

The most popular white liquor are: Maotai, and Wuliangye (high alcohol content 50% to 60 %), similar to Brandy, whisky, and Vodka; some southern Chinese drink red wine, yellow wine, or rice wine and Japanese Sake. However, beer is becoming more and more popular in every season and everywhere.

1.213 Art of tea drinking

It is indisputable that tea drinking originated in China. According to Chinese mythology, the founder of tea drinking was **Shennong (神农)** who wrote the first book on Chinese medicine. Through ages, tea drinking became an art form in the Tang Dynasty and tea ceremony as a spiritual blending of man and nature to achieve harmony and purity of the mind. However, it was Buddhism influence that tea drinking has become so pervasive in China. Hence, tea drinking is another important part of Chinese business and social entertaining.

Tea house, the public social parlors of China, have existed for several thousands years, playing especially key roles as meeting places for business and social purposes, and stop-over for travelers. Therefore, go there to drink the most common social tea drinking.

1.22 Great Leap Forward (1958—1962) (大跃进)

More, quicker, better, cheaper 多快好省

If people have more courage, the land has more grain output

人有多大胆，地有多大产

Mao Zedong initialized and led The "Great Leap Forward" with slogan of "More, quicker, better, cheaper"(多快好省) and "If people have more courage, the land has more grain output" .(人有多大胆，地有多大产) It was his political movement to industrialize China's agricultural economy rapidly to catch up with US and UK in the above short period with unrealistic goal. If implemented fearlessly, he believed that progress and its resulting abundance of goods could come in great leaps and bounds. Therefore, using cooking pot and tractors etc as raw material to melt down, every village built backyard furnace to make steel to increase steel production output. At the meantime, the farmers were collectivized into communes to uplift grain production which emphasized on ideological purity rather than expertise. Because of serious natural disasters and the withdrawal of Soviet Union technical personnel, China's agriculture was so disrupted that about 10—40 million people died of famine in the period.

The irony was: no one was responsible for the disaster mistake.

1.23 Culture Revolution (1966—1976) (文化大革命)

Because the failure of the "Great Leap Forward" weakened his position considerably in the Communist Party, and the suspicion of someone forming against him and deviating from his doctrines, it was Mao Zedong, who launched Culture Revolution which ended up destroying much of Chinese social fabric to get rid of his rivals in the Communist Party.

To Mao the Culture Revolution was a permanent political movement and constantly kept alive through unending class struggle. Hidden enemies in the party and intellectual circles had to be identified and removed. Conceived of as a "Culture Revolution to purify people's souls", the purpose of the Culture Revolution was to destroy the Four Olds—old ideas, old culture, old customs, and old habit—in order to bring the areas of education, art and literature in line with Communist ideology. Anything or anybody that was suspected of being feudal or bourgeois was to be ruined.

This political chaos that followed set back the country's economic progress, as many of its most productive and educated members were exiled to the countryside to repent their ideological sins; high schools and universities throughout the country closed down as students devoted all their time to

Red Guard activities and millions of these young students were encouraged to attack "counterrevolutionaries" and criticized those in the party who appeared to have deviated from Maoist thought; the Gang of Four, especially Jiang Qing considered anything as "Capitalism tail" and should be cut off, so the Chinese economy didn't work well. During the Culture Revolution, the number of the people who were persecuted to death was countless. The most serious confusion on the soul and spirit of the Chinese are beyond words: Neighbor turned against neighbor and family members turned on each other. No moral harmony, people suspect each other and do not trust each other any more.

Chapter2   Business

China is a land of opportunity whilst a land of risk
China is a land of opportunity whilst a land of risk

It takes longer time and bigger patience for foreigners to grasp the "Rule of the game" in China's business dealings more than you expected. Every smart western businessman has his own purpose doing business in China; however, he must be aware that the China's government use foreign business policy as a strategy to attract foreign capital, technological, and management skills through trade and economic cooperation. This will speed up China's economic development, productivity and standard of living. Therefore, the businessman must be aware of ever challenging by Chinese business practices and expectations.

Just mentioned in the preface, China is a land of opportunity whiles a land of risk. According to the <World Economic Forum>, the competitiveness goes beyond notions of exchange rate competitiveness and links the concept to productivity. Thus, competitiveness is defined as that collection of factors, policies and institutions which determine the level of prosperity that can be stained by an economy. From "Country highlights" of "The Global Competitiveness Report 2006—2007", China's ranking in 2006 has fallen from 48 (year 2005) to 54, characterized by a heterogeneous performance. On the positive side, China's buoyant growth rates coupled with low inflation, one of the highest savings rates in the world and manageable levels of public debt have boosted China's ranking on the macro-economy pillar of the GCI to 6th place —an excellent result. However, a number of structural weaknesses need to be addressed, including in the largely state-controlled banking sector. Levels of financial intermediation are low and the state has had to intervene from time to time to mitigate the adverse effects of a large, nonperforming loan portfolio. China has low penetration rates for the latest technologies (mobile telephones, Internet, personal computers), and secondary and tertiary school enrolment rates are still low by international standards. By far the most worrisome development is a marked drop in the quality of the institutional environment, as witnessed by the steep fall in rankings from 60 to 80 in 2006, with poor results across all 15 institutional indicators, and spanning both public and private institutions.

Even though the drop of ranking in institutional environment from, the temptation of 1.3 billion huge potential market and lower cost still drives global businesspeople to go to China for their business venture. However, when contemplating business prospect in China, the businessman is getting down to the nitty gritty, he soon finds that things are not what he seems to be and he must rid himself of all kinds pre—conceptions. The Chinese have their own methods of doing business and he must understand the system if he is going to get anywhere. So one way or another, he requires the minimum knowledge. And the operating environment is different from the one he is accustomed to. So a major adjustment has to be made in expectations, modes of assessment, and methods of planning and in general psychological attitudes.

International business involves many types of risk: not all can be avoided but all can, to an extent, be managed.

The risk that a firm faces when it makes a new investment comes from a number of sources: the project itself, competition, shifts in the industry, international consideration, and macroeconomic factors. Some of the risk will be eliminated by the firm over the course of multiple investments, and some will be absorbed by investors holding diversified portfolios. Now, more and more investors are risk-averse, that's why risk investments lose its value. Here I just address project risk, international considerations and macroeconomic environment because Chinese business environment is totally different with that in western. And risk of 'industry-specific' can be diversified across industries; whiles risk of competition in China is fierce from 'China marketing environment'.

2.1 Project risk

After you decide to invest in China, no matter "Capital investment project" or "Setting up an operation plant", the project-specific risk occurs when an individual project has higher or lower cash flow than expected, either because the analyst misestimated the cash flows or because of factors specific to that project. One of risks comes from the distribution of actual returns around the expected returns. Your expected cash flows or returns is totally different from actual cash flow or returns because there are so many unknowns, so many variables, and so high uncertainty in China. Most of times the actual cash flow has lower than expected cash flow for beginners hence the investment runs a loss.

2.2 International considerations
2.21 Marketing environment

At some point, many organizations recognize that their growth can only continue if they exploit overseas markets. The major challenge to companies seeking to expand overseas lies in sensitivity adapting marketing strategies that have worked at home the needs of overseas markets whose environments may be totally different to anything previously experienced.

Before undertaken a detailed market analysis, an organization should consider in general terms whether the environment of a market is likely to be attractive. By considering in general terms such matters as political stability or cultural attitudes, an organization may screen out potential markets for which it considers further analysis cannot be justified by the likelihood of success. Where an exploratory analysis of an overseas marketing environment appears to indicate some opportunities, a more details analysis might suggest important modifications to a product format that would need to be made before it could be successfully offered to the market.

2.211 First, the Chinese market is becoming extremely competitive because many companies are attempting to be the first to introduce their products to "Eat this big cake". (吃这块大蛋糕) In fact, competition has become so fierce in some industries that companies have been aggressively pursuing market share even if it means lowering their prices so they must sell at a loss. This is a game few companies can afford to play. Furthermore, penetrating the Chinese market is complicated by a variety of obstacles that prevent, slow down, or increase the cost of imported products.

Hurry, eat China this big cake

2.212 Second, hungry for western consumer's goods is a 1.3 billion potential buyers. You see a bonanza. The trouble is, as many multinational executives and ambitious entrepreneurs are soon to discover, that enormous marketplace is populated by paupers. What Beijing wants is the west to invest in modern plants applying advance technology that could use Chinese materials to make goods that could then be sold to the outside world, bringing hard currency into the national reserves. That's a fundamental difference in perspective.

2.22 Financial consideration

A firm faces this type of risk when the currency in which its earning is measured differs from the currency of its cash flow, or when it takes projects outside its domestics market. Earning and cash flows might be different than expected because of exchange rate movements or political conflict. Some of this risk may be diversified away if the firm, in the normal course of business, takes on projects in different countries and the respective currencies do not all move in the same direction. So, "Do not put all the eggs in one basket". Firms can also reduce their expose to the exchange rate component of international risk by choosing a financing mix that matches the cash flows projected for overseas venture—for instance, by borrowing money in RMB to support project in China; furthermore, given Chinese financial openness, economies with "Pegged Exchange Rates" are likely to have potentially damaging exposures which speculators may exploit; in addition, "Capital Controls" are simply part of the regulatory framework to manage Chinese own risk at both the macroeconomic and microeconomic levels.

Don't put all the eggs in one basket

Pegged Exchange Rate

Capital Control

2.3 Macroeconomic environment

Management must learn to scan the environment to determine market conditions in the countries where it is doing business or contemplating entering the market. Because of dynamic nature of political and economic events, the answers are complex—or yet to be seen and change taking place are so rapid and unpredictable. Therefore, Understanding the Chinese economic environments and markets can help managers predict how trends and events in the environments might affect their company's future performance there.

2.31 The economic environment

An organization assessing an overseas market should place great emphasis on future economic performance and the stage that a country has reached in its economic development.

Here I address three key issues for economics environment: economic growth, inflation, and surpluses and deficits. Companies would like every country in which they investing or to which they are selling to have a high growth rate in GDP and per capita GDP. From economic reform in 1979 until 2006, China GDP growth is pretty good as close to two digits; another economic factor that management needs to consider is inflation. Inflation occurs because aggregate demand is growing faster than aggregate supply. Higher inflation often results in an increase in interest rate; it is also the most significant factor that influences exchange rate. During recent 10 year (1996—2006), the inflation in China is as low as acceptable level (From 'Country highlights of China' in 'The global competitiveness report'); other measures of a country's economic stability—and potential as allocation for investment—are external and internal surplus and deficits. Managers need to monitor these balances as indicator of economic strength or weakness. Surplus rarely are a problem, but deficits are. Again, China economic stability is robust especially for export-driven strategies. There is huge surplus of import-export against US. Due to America's pressure and in-balance of surplus and deficit against US, Chinese government encourages enterprises to import high technology from US. Therefore, it is great business opportunities for those high-tech computer equipment and device, new material, and biological-gene engineering providers.

2.32 China transition

In 1978, China's government launched reforms to transform the Chinese economy away from central planning, government ownership, and import substitution policies toward greater decentralization, opening up the Chinese economy and privatization. Unlike Russia and Eastern Europe, China has gained remarkable success in this "Piecemeal social engineering" and its economy has grown dramatically.

However, the Chinese approach to transformation differs significantly from those of Russia and Eastern Europe as of "Big-bang transformation of central planned economy to market economy". The Chinese approach to economic reform and transition to market has taken place without political democratization. It continues to hold tight to totalitarian political control which initiated from Qin dynasty. Therefore, China has moved to liberalize its economy and allow private investment gradually while not completely giving up control of the economy.

The challenge facing Chinese leadership is how to maintain smooth economic growth and remove the institutional incompatibility as it continues to transition to a market economy while resisting the growing pressure to liberalize politically.

Currently, some countries, like New Zealand, Singapore have accepted China's economy as market economy. On the other hand, US, EU still consider China's economy as in transition stage from command economy.

2.33 The political environment

Political environment at local and national can affect the framework in which goods and services are marketed. Issues such as competition policy, the distribution of income and regulation vs. deregulation are essentially the result of political decisions. Marketers cannot afford to ignore developments in their political environment and must respond appropriately to such change.

The political environment is one of the less predictable elements in an organization's marketing environment. Change in political environment can result from a variety of internal and external pressures. Turbulence in the political environment can be seen by considering some of the major swings that have occurred in the political environment in the Country.

China's government is a pyramid shaped structure, from General Secretary (Hu Jintao 胡锦涛)—State Council Premier Minister (Wen Jiabao 温家宝) —State level—Provincial level—City level—Town level. State level bureaus, agencies or institutions play a critical role in administering and enforcing China's growing body of commercial and industrial law, along with its regulations on imports and exports, financial matters and in sensitive areas like intellectual property and environmental protection. Even in the most liberalized business sector in China, foreign investors entering the market will find themselves frustrated in dealing with representatives from one or more sections of China's administrative hierarchy.

Therefore, more detailed research into the laws and procedures covering the relevant business sectors or industries and the planned activities within it should enable the foreign investors to calibrate their plans to minimize the bureaucratic complication and business risk.

2.34 The social and cultural environment

Business employs, sells to, buys from, are regulated by, and owned by people. Because international business includes people from different cultures, every business function—managing a workforce, marketing output, purchasing suppliers, handling with regulators, securing funds—is subject to potential cultural problems. An international company must be sensitive to those cultural differences to predict and control its relationships and operations. Further, it should realize that its accustomed way of doing business may not be the only one or best way. When doing business in China, a company first should determine what business practices in China differ totally from those used to. Management then must decide what, if any, adjustments are necessary to operate efficiently in China.

2.35 The knowledge and information environment

China has made impressive accomplishments in economic growth and poverty reduction over the last quarter century. Now it faces daunting internal challenges such as ensuring employment to millions over the coming decades, continuing to maintain high growth, increasing its international competitiveness, and reducing income and regional inequalities. Compounding these challenges is the new knowledge and information revolution and makes effective use of knowledge in its agricultural and industrial sectors, and especially in developing its service industry. China also needs to manage the transition to an environmentally sustainable economy that better utilizes its relatively limited natural resources.

Knowledge and Information is a crucial to organizations in the analysis for their environment. Information about the current status of the environment is used as a starting point for planning future marketing strategy, based on assumptions about how the environment will change. It is also vital to monitor the implementation of an organization's marketing plans and to note the cause of any deviation from plan and to identify whether this is caused by internal or external environmental factors. Marketing information allows management to improve its strategy planning, tactical implementation of programs and its monitoring and control. In turbulent marketing environment, having access to timely and relevant information can give a firm a competitive advantage. This can be manifested, for example, in the ability to spot turning points in the business cycle ahead of competitors; to respond more rapidly to consumers' changing preferences; and to adapt manufacturing schedules more closely to demand patterns, thereby avoiding the build up of inventories.

2.36 The technological environment

An analysis of the technological environment of an overseas market is important for organizations that require the use of a well-developed technical infrastructure and a workforce that is able to use technology. Communications are an important element of technological infrastructure—poorly developed telephone and postal communications may inhibit attempts to make credit cards more widely available, for instance.

The primary goal of mastering the transition to the knowledge and information based economy is to raise the technological level of the Chinese economy. In addition to establishing the foundations of: updating economic incentives and institutions, investing in human capital, and building the information infrastructure, the focus here can be put in the perspective of improving the Chinese innovation system. It should be clear, however, that innovation is to be understood as products, process, practices that are new in the local context of China, down to the different regions and localities.

First is the strong need for more effective and expanded policies aiming at the diffusion of new technologies throughout the economy. Next, the improvement of the domestic research and development effort, affected both by a questionable combination of an excessive market-based approach and top-down conceptions of government programs. Finally considered are several ways for China to more effective exploit global knowledge, especially by making better use of foreign investment, the most efficient means to raise the technological performances of the economy in the short and medium runs.

However, a major obstacle is the poor capability of transforming scientific and technological advances into practical productive forces; China's exceptionally poor technical regulations and standards are major obstacles to proper diffusion of modern technology and know-how; high-technology parks have been growing very fast but technology diffusion beyond the parks has been limited. From 2006—2007 "The Global Competitiveness report", you know, the China's "Technological Readiness" ranking is 75 out of 125.

The Chinese government is committed to building the telecommunications networks and strategic information systems that enable widespread access to information and communication. However, the telecom legal and regulatory environment has not kept up with the major changes in the telecommunications sector; Chinese telecom markets still have to be liberalized and deregulated; China Telecom needs to continue its tariff rebalancing effort to prepare for the introduction of competition in basic service.

2.4 Legal barrier

> Nowadays, judges can be bribed for RMB 500,000 yuan, the government should learn from 包公

Shen Baokui: a vegetable wholesaler

In the good old Confucian way, we expect government to be benevolent rulers and to love the people as their sons. We expect them to be honest, and we say, "Go ahead, spend what you like out of the public finds, and we will not demand a public budget or a rending of public accounts". So, the Chinese conception of government is known as "Parental government", therefore, there is no much difference about "Rule by law" or "Rule by man". However, Han Feizi (The first one who pioneered systematic Legal system in China) advocated that Legalist conception of government should be by Constitution rather than by persons.

So, in a philosophy of moral harmony rather than a philosophy of force environment, Legal environment is another important factor to be considered. Because in such a turbulent business and fierce competitiveness environment, legal is one of key factors to protect your business prospect. The critical question is: Does the judicial system allow for the reasonable, expeditions, transparent, and low-cost settlement of disputes, or is justice for sale? Well, China has voluminous regulations, but enforcement and interpretation are arbitrary and depend on the point that authorities are trying to make at any given time. Therefore, there is no more Bao Gong（包公）who was a symbol of justice and integrity in China any more. That's why a complaint from one vegetable wholesaler named Shen Baokui: "Nowadays, judges can be bribed for RMB500, 000 yuan, the government should learn from "Bao Gong" from "South China Morning Post" on September 21, 2006. Indeed, the China's judiciary is often criticized by ordinary people and overseas analysis for lacking independence and professionalism. Judges are appointed by local governments and answer directly to them. Many magistrates are poorly trained and corrupt repeatedly. The legal system in those days was actually not as good as the one we have now. Judges back then also served as prosecutors and decided everything on their own, so it was easy to have unjust rulings.

Today, commercial practices are still subject to ever-changing rules and regulations that are interpreted differently at different times. It is lose-lose situation for both foreign and Chinese investors unless they are under the protection of powerful personals.

2.5 The Accounting system

Political, cultural, legal and economic force, together with the firm's sources of capital affects each country's philosophy and attitude towards its accounting system. They also lead to the country's accountants treating accounting issues differently. These differing treatments in turn impact on a firm's reported profits or loss, the values of asset, its tax payable and its decision to begin, or to continue, to operate in the country. International businesses that rely on foreign accounting records but fail to recognize these differences may make expensive, perhaps fatal, strategic errors and operating mistakes.

The accounting system used by China's state-owned enterprises, which is a modification of the system used in the former Soviet Union not GAAP (Generally Accepted Accounting Principles), is designed to provide information about an enterprise's aggregate production. This information is then passed from the enterprise to the central governors so that they can monitor the enterprise's success in fulfilling its performance goals in the economy's central plan and can make mid-plan adjustments as needed. Therefore, international businesses must approach financial statements developed in its system with great caution.

The China's accounting systems are of little used to international businesses trying to meet their own internal managerial and reporting requirements. These systems focus on recording production information needed by central governors but ignore "trivialities' such as revenues, costs, and profits that may be incompatible with prevailing or past ideologies that determined the form of enterprises reporting.

CPA(certified public accountant) is new but now becoming more and more popular in China, however, most accounts still work in companies and report the accounting system according to the managerial requirements unless they do not want the job. That's why so many companies have two sets even three sets accounting report system. One is for internal, the other for external.

2.6 The Audit system

There is a China's National Audit Office which established in 1983. According to an Auditor-General Li Jinhua's (李金华) speech in a seminar (one essay from "People Daily Online" on August 23, 2003): "Although great improvements have been made, China's audit work still lags behind that of the developed countries in content, methods and information release because our auditing system still depends on outdated hand-checking, and we do not have a regular release of auditing reports. All these things clearly hamper the development of our auditing work. So far, the office has mainly focused on the legitimacy of the use of fiscal funds, and we do not have a complete auditing system capable of uncovering deep fiscal problems. By 2007, the office will open all auditing and investigation reports to the public, except for those concerning State secrets".

So, Chinese previous Premier Zhu Rongji (朱镕基) appreciated the National Audit office did a good job in helping to maintain order in the economy through detecting and curbing fraudulent activities such as accounting frauds, contributing to the country's fight against corruption and its efforts to build a clean government and to ensure a healthy economic development, and called for the improvement of auditing of taxation and finance departments and of leading State-owned enterprises, in order to increase revenue, safeguard financial security and prevent the loss of State assets. For example, in year 2003, The National Audit Office audited China Construction Bank and Agricultural Development Bank of China and their branches nationwide and uncovered evidence used in the prosecution of 51 economic crime cases, which involved 74 bank officials and RMB 2.274 billion (US$274 million).

Maybe the Audit system needs to be improved or maybe there are too many cases to be audited. The key issue is lacking the independence and professionalism. The auditors are appointed by governments and of course answer to them directly. Let's look at the irony matter: the corruption cases happened in China, but China Audit Office can not find out those corruption cases however foreign audit department can find out. According to an essay of Chinese Magazine <World Knowledge> (July/2006), in 500,000 corruption cases in China, 64% related to international trading or foreign enterprise in China. For instance, according <Foreign Corrupt Practices Act of 1997>, The Audit department from US found out that one of U.S based company had bribed state-own doctors more than RMB 162.3 million in year 2005 and asked the company to take action against senior officers in China. Because most foreign companies can not win market competition and gain profit due to pure competitive advantage such as, technology advancement and pricing advantage. So, they bribed senior government officers by: providing overseas training (it can be said traveling and sight-seeing), sponsoring their children to study in oversea, and co-building EMBA program for senior managers etc hidden means.

2.7 Corruption

It is not only corrupt people's money to their purse

but also corrupt people's future and growing opportunities of the country

The government has quite openly admitted that there is too much corruption in the country. Officials using inside information to manipulate incipient Chinese stock exchanges and make insider profits on business deal; Financial speculation using public or company funds, building up paper profits that can turn into real losses, which then get charged to the entities they represent. So, the question is no longer

who is but who is not corrupt? Together with the emergence
of Triad and organized crime, these developments are tearing
up the fabric of the nation. The more serious is: Corruption is
extending to not only public sectors, but also to private
sectors, or can be said widespread to every corner. The latest
report on September 25,2006 from China's Xinhua news
agency, said Mr. Chen Lianyu (陈良宇) was fired as Secretary
of the Shanghai Municipal Committee for corruption
discovered in a probe into misuse of Shanghai's RMB 10
billion ($1.25 billion) pension fund for his clique's interest and
other corruptions such as "helping further the economic
interests of illegal business people, protecting staff who
severely violated laws and discipline, furthering the interests
of family members by taking advantage of his official posts".
It is a political fight about Hu Jintao against Jiang Zhemin to
strengten and secure Hu's power, another reason maybe is
continuous preasure from national people due to internet
exposure.

Corruption distorts decision-making, which hurts
competition, market efficiency, and economic development. It
is not only corrupt people's money to their purse but also
corrupt people's future and growth opportunity of country. In
many countries, a small payment to government officials, such
as customs officers, immigration authorities or building
inspectors, is an accepted part of doing business. International
businesspeople who want to succeed in such countries are
often faced with the ethical problem of whether or not to
make such payments. For example, U.S, UK, Canada, and
Australia etc do not allow such payment, so, international
businesspeople from those countries face dilemma. If not, the
relative process time maybe longer even result unknown; if
yes, they will breach <Foreign Corrupt Practices Act of
1997> (for U.S).

Every Chinese hates corruption but must cope with it for
his own interest. Because corruption has its deep-rooted in

Chinese culture of history which initiated from totalitarian politics and "parental government". The China's government did take some actions to stop it to build clean government and healthy economy environment. However, the result is not desirable. If this phenomenon continues or worsens, maybe the Chinese economy will lose its continuous growing opportunities and all the previous results and effort of reform will be ruined.

2.8 Hiring staff

> **Hire the right people to do the right thing in the right time at the right place**

After you decide to set up an operation plant in China, the next is to get the talent people. Everyone knows to "Hire the right people to do the right thing in the right time at the right place". In practical, maybe it does not work. Even you seem to hire the right people as paper required however you do not satisfy his performance. If hiring westerner, the advantage is that they can manage the company in your way. However, the biggest challenge is that your plant operating in such different and complex environment. Does your Chinese staff follow him? Does your business partner, such as customers, suppliers, or government agencies cooperate with him? Obviously not always, there are so many failure cases that not working well; if you employ local Chinese, another trouble arises. First is language, it is not easy for you to hire someone who has management expertise with good English; second, the headache is management style, do you accept Chinese management style in your plant or you want to send him overseas to get training then he changes another job; third, is credit or merit check. From resume, you can screen and check his background and reference, the question is: Is his reference objective or not? If not, maybe you lose the chance to hire a good staff; furthermore, for criminal check, only Shanghai and Beijing are available for limited check if you want to hire staff only from these two cities; in addition, you can't get your credit report in China because currently there is no such system. So, it is a potential risky to hire local talent. Another alternative is to hire those who earn overseas related degree, get similar oversea working experience.

You try to get honest and smart staff. But how can an employer predict what will guide a person's moral compass in the future under a variety of situation? Some of the situations can be predicted since they are part of the job. Other situations cannot be predicted. In the future, a person may undergo sudden life change or stress may tempt dishonesty, especially in Chinese turbulence environment. Or, a supervisor may ask an employee to participate in a questionable act, such as document shredding, where there is an element of coercion or an implicit threat they would lose their job if they do not cooperate. Part of complication is to discover ahead of time how a person may react when ordered to do something dishonest.

2.81 Spy staff

Most western employers wish to hire employee who has ambition to keep company grow. If your operation is labor-intensive, maybe is fine. However, if you product has some technological advancements, pay more attention to your key staff because it seems every Chinese keens on his own business or 'quick-to-success'. Take more time to check his background and monitor his behavior in right way. If you do not care about your technology advantage or potential competitor, that's not the case. For instance, one CTO from previous famous DVD Player took all the key staff and set up another DVD plant, built another DVD brand, as a result: the former DVD plant bankrupted. On the other hand, your critical database, such as customers, suppliers, and finance maybe are another target. Therefore, be careful about engaging some Chinese staff for their purpose, however loyal they have proved themselves to be in the past or when working for you outside China.

2.9 Some tips to improve your business prospects

2.91 Business Cards

Take plenty of your business cards when travel to China. If no, you mean nothing. You can have any form of your card. Ensure that one side is in English and the other is in Chinese. Do not print your name in red because red means blood or death in Buddhist tradition. However, your name printed in gold ink is welcome because in Chinese business culture, gold is the color of prestige and prosperity.

2.92 The Contract

Insist on detailed contract, preferably executed in an independent jurisdiction in the third country. Because Chinese hate detailed contracts, they much prefer contractual terms broad enough to allow constant "between-the-lines" interpretation, usually in their favor.

2.93 Face

Now you know face is very important for face-conscious of Chinese, because giving face earns respect and loyalty, and it should be done whenever the situation warrants.

> **Everyone wishes to be "A Great Man"**

- Don't insult or criticize someone in front of others
- Don't ask Chinese not to smoke if they smoke. You will be considered very rude if you do so
- Don't treat someone as an underling when someone in an organization is high
- Praise someone sincerely: for his job well-done in front of peers or superiors, for his cooperation, for his assistance, because 'Everyone wishes to be "A Great Man"'

•Help someone to avoid an embarrassing situation
•Please someone in entertainment occasions: For instance, when playing golf, try your best however, you still lose just one or two holes; when playing majong, lose money to them by saying you are beginner but interested in playing; in dining, drinks much and seems drunk. All of these, you must show in your heart, do not let them know you do it deliberately. Give them sufficient face then you will get business prospect.

2.94 Guanxi

Guanxi, is an undefined linkage of relatives, close friends, colleges and what in the west would be the connections. If you have it, you are going to get special treatment. Your contract will be signed without great loss of time and effort in negotiations. You will find raw material provided and deadlines met. All problems will be smoothed over.
•Study in top MBA business school in your home university if you get the chance, your business success is not far, because a lot of Chinese senior minister's children or senior officials in there. And Chinese consider relationship of classmate is the most purity.
•Go to source: attend trade show in Western or China, get business card as many as you can. You are on the right track.
•Find a matchmaker: make contacts to Chinese associates as mutual friends as intermediary
•Show your patience to any business negotiation or argument
•Do not make any enemy even you have any conflict, argument or bad experience, give you or your counterpart a leeway
•Build on the trustworthiness of the individual or the company, if a company promised certain things and delivered as promised, the company is showing trustworthiness and the Chinese would be more inclined to deal with them again
•Contact frequently with each other to foster understanding and emotional bonds and the Chinese often feel obligated to do business with their friends first

2.95 Psychological analysis

Most business deal done with what? Technology advantage, cost leadership, or brand awareness? No, psychology takes the significant role. Because we are human, we have weakness. So, do analyze your business partner psychology: money, women or other personal trait. Attack his personal weakness to get what you want. Do you still remember "Lai Changxing"'s(赖昌兴) case? This guy has got only primary school education; however, he has business talent and is excellent in "Psychological analysis". Either those senior officials from local, provincial, or central government trapped in his money, women or others to help him to smuggle or avoid tax payment more than RMB 30 billion. One of the officials did not like money and women. Through Lai's thoroughly investigation from his relatives and friends, Lai knew that he liked "oil painting". So, Lai bought it from Italy and sent to him, finally Lai got the deal. That's why nowadays a lot of Chinese businessmen have learned from him to build "Red mansion" (红楼) to corrupt government officials, called **"Red mansion phenomenon" (红楼现象)**. Another interesting example was: One "Farmer Entrepreneur" had a successful food production and possessed his own brand. However, his embarrassing occasion is his education level, only primary. His customer analyzed the situation with previous unsuccessful deal and brought the professor from top university to negotiate the deal. Finally his customer got the order. Why? Very simple, everyone needs to be respected and wishes to be "A Great Man".

2.96 Tax

Tax system in China is still imperfect. Some reasons maybe the system itself, ineffective audit administration system, or independent accountant system (CPA is new in China).

Accountability and transparency are the key problems for their accounting systems, that's why so many anti-dumping cases against China? It is common for company to have two even three sets accounting system. That's why so many foreign enterprises are still operating or expanding in China even running a loss? This is another opportunity for your business.

2.97 Crisis management

The crisis management is another crucial part of your business because higher uncertainty there. If you can not manage properly, it can strike a company in many ways such emergencies are unexpected incidents where damage or injury occurs. Those who have the task of managing a crisis must not only behave in a correct business like manner under stress, the general public also demands an immediate statement on the matter.

For example, major accident in your plant or customer's site, interruption of part supply, industrial dispute, and road accident etc, all of those will affect your plant smooth operation. So, set up a "Crisis committee", plan detail, train the relative staff (for dealing with journalists as well as passing on the relevant information to employees with special responsibility such as plant operators, drivers, security staff and switchboard operators), and have alternatives. In case of emergency, everyone must know what he/she has to do and to whom he/she has to report.

2.98 Dispute

Law pays attention to evidence not truth

When you are a hard-headed and tough, or are infuriated by constant delays and arguments, or refuse to bow to blackmail and threats, such disputes are likely to be spectacular. However, just mentioned in 'Legal barrier", most of time, legal system is unfavorable to you. If you want to fight, consider those headache problems: Law pays attention to evidence not truth, so how to collect evidences? Who will be

44

your witness because you are a foreigner? The best way are: cooperate as possible, talk to top ranks of the Chinese leadership; if things are unsatisfactory, hit the headlines in the international press; finally, the higher possibility you pack bags and go home to minimize your loss.

2.99 Hiring Staff

Hire those staff that will bring business prospect to you. For example, there is high demand of high-tech electronics equipment and device, therefore, hire the secretary of Minister or department manager from National Import department with broad network and offer them with attractive package such as stock option and 401K etc besides salary. If you can get them, your order will coming like snow-flaking.

Chapter3   Outsourcing

China is an intriguing market and one well worth investigating from a number of perspectives. For buyers China can provide a wide range of quality goods at highly competitive prices. It is a major producer of textile, apparel, and footwear; foodstuffs; a wide range of machinery; metals and metal products; chemicals; raw materials; toys, games, and sporting goods; electrical appliance, electronics device, computer and its accessories; and handcrafts, among many other items. Its business can handle orders ranging from the smallest to the largest. That's why China is called **"Global Manufacturing Hub"**.

Like marketing, many organizations rush to China to pursue market share in this fierce competitive marketing environment, now many organizations hasten to China for outsourcing to reduce cost. In an effort to sustain competitive advantage, many leading companies from Microsoft to Nike and GM, are incorporating outsourcing into their management decision-making to reduce cost, increase productivity, innovation and service, and generate higher return for shareholders. Those small to medium enterprises (SME) operating within a highly competitive market, with no significant differentiating capacities, pursuing a cost strategy may well be appropriate. However, outsourcing is one of the most complex and controversial issues in business today. Transformational outsourcing isn't right for every company because it is a socio-technical phenomenon. Therefore, outsourcing is transformational to the organization and requires attention to not only the social and human but also technology impacts that accompany business transformation. It represents a major strategic commitment. Evaluate the risks and rewards, determine what and how to outsource, select the right grower, and put the right team together to make it work.

3.1 Rewards

Rapidly changing and increasing complex business issues are creating key shifts in organizations and the manner in which they do business. The advance of technology, the sophistication of business operations, and the need for constant growth are circumstances that suggest a focus on functional core competencies. As companies struggle to adapt to and keep up with the demands of customers and shareholders alike, that focus on core competencies may suggest outsourcing as a potential strategy to remain competitiveness.

●Transfer the responsibility and the risk for the delivery and enhance an integrated operational service
●Focus on core business
●Reduce and control operating cost
●Reduce labor cost
●Balance competitive pressure
●Gain access to world-class capabilities
●Improve time to market and so on

3.2 Risks

However, if you organizations have a poor strategy, a lack of leadership, many misconceptions, unrealistic expectations of success, incomplete planning, or just because of Force, preasure from shareholders or the board without first proving that outsourcing is the best business solution, a result of the fast and furious trying to get contracts signed, all of these will lead a risk to fail. Therefore, executives and managers of organization must be vigilant about risk avoidance and mitigation. Here I address the most risks concerned except project risks and legal risks which mentioned in business section.

3.21 The loss of intellectual property rights (IPR)

Most businesses have a significant amount of sensitive information, including patent, intellectual property, trade

47

secret, or sensitive material etc. Therefore, safeguarding those critical business information security and privacy, including theft by company insiders, former employees, and computer hackers abound must be completely addressed. Off-shore outsourcing presents different because legal standards and business practices governing whether and how sensitive information should be guarded vary around the world.

3.22 Confidentiality leaks

By introducing more "outsiders" into its affairs, organizations increase the likelihood of there being a leak of important information.

3.23 Vendor risks

Vendor business practices can vary greatly around the world especially in complication of China; furthermore, to get the contract signed, most Chinese vendors will overstate their competencies and exaggerate the business and technical certifications they posses and the clients they serve; in addition, vendors may suffer short-term difficulties or go on liquidation to interrupt your supply. Maybe the most difficulty is being leveraged by your vendor due to poor contract or limited supplier market options. Therefore, read your vendors intentions and select them carefully in vendor selection process.

3.24 Delivery risks

A major issue facing organizations that choose to outsource involves delivery: the delivery of quality products or services, on time, within the scope of the contract, yet allowing for growth and innovation. If you have a great product with a great cost base, but your outsourcing initiative can not deliver on time; or if your vendor can get product to market, but the product lacks quality, hence your customers will fill their product needs elsewhere, and your outsourcing initiative will fail.

3.25 Human resource risks

Most of concern is labor related issues. For example, your vendors employ child workers, breach labor-law to work too long (for example, more than 12 hours a day), provide poor working environment, or can not pay the minimum wage etc.

3.26 Force Majeure risks

These are the most difficult to predict and specify. What is the likelihood of a war, hurricane, or earthquake? Yet these risks can be estimated with some measure of objectivity, and an appropriate mitigation strategy can be developed and enacted. Business monitor (www.businessmonitor.com) provides extensive coverage of the political, economic, and military risks that exist for countries around the world.

3.3 Audit

Let's start from the position that your organization has established its strategy and clearly understand its strategic imperatives, and transformation is on the agenda.

In order to create early and sustainable growth through outsourcing, you must pick a vendor who knows what to do it, how to do it, how well to do it, and how quickly to do it. A complex process at best, vendor selection involves defining detailed business requirements, developing a business model and delivery model, developing an 'Request For Information' or 'Request For Proposal' document, evaluating and selecting vendors, conducting due diligence, including management interviews and site visits, finalizing the operating model, creating the governance structure, and finally negotiating the contract and "Service-Level Agreement".

To start a search, network within your industry for referrals, read trade publications, use the Internet, or engage a consultant to assist in research. After you finish your search and select as more vendors as possible, do as follows:
●Include a realist description of your expectations for the relationship, and ask the vendor how it intends to fulfill these expectations.

•Ask for the information on vendor's management capability, customer relationship management, reporting, and policy or procedural compliance, and verify them on site visit.

•State your quality monitoring and reporting requirements, and ask if all the elements required (equipment, human resources, and process) are present in the vendor's current program.

•Request for quotation: including detail BOM cost, labor cost, and overhead that might associate with the project, so you can better compare vendors in the final stages of your selection process.

Here I list the key audit check lists for your considerations, how to weight for every item based on your organization.

1. Experience and expertise: How long has this vendor been in this business, and what similar project experience does this vendor have?

2. Quality: Their quality standards, including QA, QC, Quality manual and procedure. The most important is how to make it to achieve your quality requirements; relative quality certificate, such as ISO 9000, TS 16949, UL, TUV etc based on different industries special requirements.

3. Integrity: Confidentiality, security, intellectual property rights norms, business model.

4. Price and margin: Quote at a competitive price, potential to reduce it every year.

5. Financial strength: Does the vendor's financial standing, and stability support the significant investment you will make, or is it start-up or thinly capitalized?

6. Flexibility. Business model, contract, and scalability

3.4 Quality

It used to be only large corporations and multinational corporations that faced global competition; now even small companies are affected, especially for technology advancement. Advances in communication technology have made people from all over the world electronics neighbors and electronics customers, advances in transportation technology allows raw materials produced in one country to be used in the manufacture of the products in a second country that are, in turns, sold to end users in a third country. So, today no company is immune to the effects of global competition. To compete globally, they have to produce goods of world-class quality, which meant producing better goods at reasonable, competitive prices.

However, quality perception in China is different from westerns. The basis of many complaints by foreigners outsourcing business in China is the lack of quality control. They complaint the attitude "near enough is good enough" is widespread throughout the country. But goods produced using this work philosophy is certainly not good enough for most end-users; moreover, to produce quality goods or service, it needs all the staff's effort and support. However, in China, quality seems only issue for quality department.

So, successful outsourcing is dependent on how well you define your customer requirements and how well your measure how those requirements are being met. If you can not define or measure your requirements, you are doomed to fail. Especially in China, you must be specific and deliberate documenting your expectations for quality. Second, when audit on site, check quality control procedure and relative record more carefully.

3.5 Lead time

Just mentioned in risk section above, if your vendor cannot deliver the quality product on time within the scope of contract, the outsourcing is not working. The serious is: you may lose your customers potentially. So, assess your vendor's lead time in every angle: their capacity planning, physical space and equipment, skilled staff, availability of raw material, their sub-contractors, and logistics forward carrier etc. If something wrong with one of the factors may affect the delivery. Moreover, evaluate your vendor's ability to ramp up when you need them. So, you must identify their ability to increase staff and skills to react to your needs.

3.6 Managing your outsourcing vendor

While vendor performance is the certainly critical to the success of an outsourcing program, perhaps of even greater importance is the management of the ongoing relationship once the contract is signed. Because the success or failure of an outsourcing activity is not dependent only on the criteria used to make the outsourcing decision. Process and systems are needed to manage the new organizational relationship and control the outsourcing operations.

In many situations, the relationships between an organization and an outsourcer resemble a partnership, rather than traditional customer-supplier relationships. In these relationships, developing close co-operative relationships can be an important contributor to the success of the outsourcing venture.

3.61 The Contract

Typically, the contract specifies the obligations that each party has to the other, performance indicators and financial arrangements, procedures to be undertaken in the event of a dispute, and provisions for termination.

The contract allows both parties to consider the nature of the relationship in the new undertaking, and specifies the ground rules at the start of the relationship. However, it is difficult to include all of the important aspects within the contract, as it becomes too cumbersome and inflexible. In addition, it is difficult to foresee all contingences that may arise over the course of the relationship and include them within the formal agreement. Therefore, the contract is only the staring point in setting up systems to manage the outsourcing relationship.

3.62 IPR

Therefore, provide the vendor with an explicitly stated license to use the IPR only in order to comply with their obligation under the contract and throughout any termination process, verify the vendor's data security/protection measure, investigate the vendor's security practice, to ensure they're as robust as you require. Document your requirements and define in details the methods and integration with your vendors.

3.63 The conflict points

There will be points of conflict involving such as: unrealistic expectations of the buyer due to over-pledging during sales process, contradictory interests of the buyer and the vendor, and so on. These flashpoints must be monitored and communicated upward through the organization, and must be reported back to the vendor on a regular basis in an effort to make the necessary shifts to accomplish the goals. The focus here is on the solution, so that the working relationship stays healthy and respectful.

3.64 Performance

It has been suggested that an organization may gain control over the functions being outsourced through ongoing monitoring of the work performance, as well as monitoring aspects of the outsourcing relationship throughout the contract period. This may be achieved through the use of performance measures and benchmarks which focus on areas such as, delivery responsiveness, product quality and cost, customer satisfaction. These may be included in the contract, or may be negotiated at a later time.

3.65 Cultural differences

The big challenge for you is to manage the remote team. These include geographically separated, across time zones, across functions, and with diverse cultural foundations, so, problems are inevitable. The potential for cultural clashes rises exponentially. Never underestimate what it will take to address these differences and do what you must to avoid misunderstandings, for examples, religion, mode of dress, and social practices in the country.

To be culturally aware, therefore, open the doors to communication of critical information early and clearly, so that organizations and their outsourcing vendors can be more effective, avoiding misunderstandings or offending others, and building relationships that are critical to success.

3.66 Contingencies

What happens if the vendor, in spite of carefully developed plans and a professional drafted contract, fails, for one reason or another, to deliver? Although such failures are exceptions, they do occur, even with the superb quality methodologies of most offshore vendors. Assess the implications of vendor failure: What are the business performance implications?

3.7 Some tips to improve your outsourcing more successfully

- No rush to outsourcing, plan carefully
- Set up the project team, select capable manager with understanding insightful Chinese culture
- Build "Vendor selection team"
- Set your expectations more specific, measurable, and attainable
- Select your vendor strictly based on "A, B, C" rating system, select A for preferred vendor, B for qualified vendor, C for coached vendor
- Select at least three vendors only this you have enough bargaining power about quality, deliver time and price
- Evaluate your vendor on an annual basis because the situation can be changed, such as A can be downgraded to B due to poor quality, delivery and service etc
- Negotiate effectively and draw up watertight contracts
- Allow the sufficient time for transition, because the transition period---that is, the period between vendor selection and beginning operations with your new vendor—is critical. There will be no cost savings, but rather significant expenses, during this period.

●Monitor the lead time and quality progress on a regular basis. For saving cost, use e-mail and web-conference if necessary.

●Outsource non-critical part or component in China, if not, the intellectual property rights are the big concern because a lot of Chinese companies do not pay attention to them seriously. Even your vendor knows them, but they can not guarantee their vendor's integrity; moreover, the current Chinese "Efficiency Enhancer" is still below average just 71 (from 2006 competitiveness report, the "Technology Readiness" rating was 75 out of 125 countries); in addition, you will lose your technical expertise. If you think it is OK for outsourcing critical part or component in China, for critical data and vendor's quality certificates, test and verify every data carefully in your home side, if not, there is a potential problem there.

●Pay attention to seasonable power shortage during Jun—Aug, Dec—Feb when schedule your delivery time from China. Because most family use air-con in summer to cool down whiles in winter to warm up, so the state power authority stops to supply power to companies 3 to 4 days per week; moreover, "Spring festival" means a lot for Chinese, because most workers from northern go home to celebrate about one month due to shortage of train ticket.

Chapter4   LIFE

Since life is something more than a game, it is always full of difficulties. It is a unity because it has grown out of the difficulties of early life and out of the striving for a goal. The Chinese are a race of pragmatists. And they are opportunists as well. They have stayed alive and thrived under varying degree of oppression, hardship and privation for more than 5,000 years. To them, life is about making the best of what is materially available in any given situation. They live and die in the quest for fortune and fame, which essentially means uplifting the family name. To stay in the running, they must resort to all means, fair and foul.

All the problems of life are at bottom social problems. We see social problems expressed in the nursery, the school, in friendship, in politics, in economic life, and so on. We have seen that social maladjustment is caused by the social consequences of the sense of inferiority and the striving for superiority.

Dark, broken promise, lying, the soured dream, people haven't found meaning in their lives and feel that the world is not interested at all, so they're running all the time looking for it. They think the next car, the next house, the next job. Then they found things are empty, too, and they keep running. However once you start running, it's hard to slow yourself down.

4.1 Love

The emperor preferred the beauty than the country

"Ai jiang shan geng ai mei ren" (爱江山更爱美人) (The emperor preferred the beauty than the country). Indeed, Love, is beautiful, is holy. No matter in ancient or modern, east or west, there are so many love stories. Everyone wishes to get it even sacrifice one's life. However, now it is changed, love is not pure one, people in love with partner not means in love with life, in love with trust, in love with mutual support. It mixes others, such as social status, personality, look, fortune, fitness etc because only love is not enough to get quality of life. Maybe you will argue: First sight love is true love. No, most of time it is not, it is based on appearance, or love perception, is it unconditional love? So, people often ask: Is there any true love in the world? What's my Mr. Right or Ms. Right? Even love each other at the beginning, how long can last? The reason is: Love is simple, but living together is not easy (相爱简单，相处太难)

Here the big difference is that you want to pursue love to marry or you want to trade in. Sometimes it is very difficult to tell because we are civilians and not so wise to see through it at the beginning. Only through marriage, as times being, then you will know your life partner's real intention. How long it depends? Finally, maybe you are the victim.

4.2 Marriage

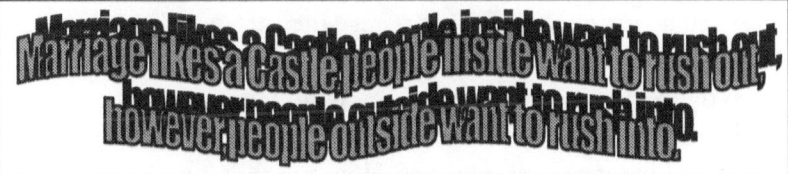

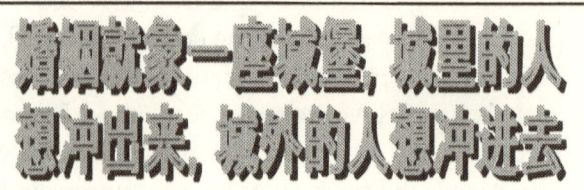

婚姻就象一座城堡，城里的人
想冲出来，城外的人想冲进去

Marriage likes a Castle, people inside want to rush out however people outside want to rush in （婚姻就象一座城堡，城里的人想冲出来，城外的人想冲进去）. It is the key point of book **<Wei Cheng>** 《围城》 from famous Chinese writer Qiang Zhongshu. Marriage, almost I knew everyone had a problem with it. Some have problem getting into it, some had problem getting out. In this materialistic culture, everyone seems to struggle with the commitment, as if it were crocodile from some murky swamp. They don't know what they are themselves—so how can they know who they are marrying. That's why there are a great many dealing with love stories, but we find few books dealing with happy marriages.

In this culture, it's so important to find a loving relationship with someone because so much of the culture does not give them that. Therefore in today's materialistic society, either they're too selfish to take part in a real loving relationship, or they rush into marriage for something or because of force and then several months later, get divorce. Even those couples seem happy outside, but what's inside? Maybe in the beginning, they have similar belief and value. However, as life goes on they change expectations. So, how long will they keep loving relationship? Some do not divorce, not mean they love each other, but they want to keep their social status or face. Why, because they are selfish, ego, or self-centered. They hope life partner love them, compromise to them in every life details, not betray them. However, do they love their partner in whole life? Do they make any commitment to their partner? How can they ask their partner like that? And can they do that in their whole life? Probably not, that's why so many sex scandals or ultra-marriage loves, so many prostitutes or Red Light areas.

China's GDP per capital is below two thousand US dollar; it is still considered a poor country. To breach poverty, the best, fastest and easiest way is marriage. That's why so many beautiful women married western people no matter love or not, cultural background. She can have quality of life for herself, even her family, the price is sham marriage. From culture section you know, Chinese consider them as a family unit not as a free individual, so it is their obligation to help their family members or relatives to gain fame. There was a beautiful legend about "Shaojun chu sai" (绍君出塞) (using one of the four great beauties to exchange peace between two countries in ancient China). And Chinese government often uses it as material to educate patriotism.

If you are lucky you get a life partner just of pure love. Unfortunately this is seldom the case. You marry someone; you marry her whole family even friends. After she get "Green card", she ask your help for her family member, for example, her sister or brother want to study in US, can you sponsor them? My parents have never been to US, can you apply social visit for them? "Honey, my best friend wants to study in US, please help me to sponsor him" ...... It is endless. Hence, you must get well along not only with her, but also her family members. Finally, you break up probably. The reason is: we have different culture background and personality and I paid the heavy price with my marriage. So, what do you want to say?

4.3 Family

In the Confucian social and political philosophy we see a direct transition from the family, jia, to the state, guo, as successive stages of human organization, as in such saying "When the family is orderly, then the state is peaceful", thus the doctrine of filial piety is the cornerstone of all ethics in The Analects of Confucius. Indeed, if no family, there is no foundation, no secure ground, upon which people may stand today. Therefore, it becomes clear to me as I've been sick or in festive season. If you don't have the support, love, caring, and concern that you get from, you don't have anything.

Family in Chinese term, called "Jia" (家), which generally means the basic family group, those who are related by blood, marriage, or adoption, living and managing their family fame together. Every member of the Jia works together for its common objective: sustaining and increasing the Jia's wealth and social status. However, love is so supremely important in the family. Love each other or treasure. This is part of what a family is about, not just love, but letting others know there's someone who is watching out for you---'spiritual security'. Exactly, when you are tired, broken heart, or despair, Jia is the only way to pacify your spiritual need. Friends are great, but friends are not going to be here on a night when you're coughing and can't sleep and someone has to sit up all night with you, comfort you, and try to be helpful. That's why family is so important for everyone.

There is no experience like having children. That's all. There is no substitute for it. You cannot do it with a friend. You cannot do it with a lover. If you want the experience of having complete responsibility for another human being, and learn how to love and bond in the deepest way, then you should have children. Furthermore, children are a good bond of maintaining your marriage. If you do not have love foundation, it is no point for the "Empty shell marriage". However, when some Chinese girls want to get something through sham marriage, family is not the reason. Having a children means they will lose their negotiating terms for another marriage.

4.4 Money:

> **Money can't give you happnless, but no money you are definitely no happy**

Money can not give you happiness, but no money you are definitely not happy. Do you agree with that? See, everything in this world must pay, food, clothing, utility bill, insurance etc, from your birth to death. So, people are struggle for money.

But, people just do not satisfy with their need, they want more. Social status, power, and love, can they get all of those? Most of not, so, they wish money as a substitute.

Why they work so hard to get accomplishment, they hope to get bigger pay check. Because only money is real, they can control it as they want, buy not only material things, such as luxury house, nice car, and elegant dress, but also a longer life, better education, more health care, and even civil and political rights, eat delicious food, go fun vocation etc. They are content with materialistic satisfaction but money can not satisfy their spiritual need and is not a reliable route of happiness. Only below the poverty line does money bring well-being, above it, increases in personal wealth do not bring increased happiness. So, what's next, finally they become a slave of money and not happy at all. Can they bring it to the tomb?

4.5 Accomplishment

In this world, there are only two kinds of people: Winner and Loser

Need refers to something that is deep rooted in an individual's personality. From Marlow's hierarchy of needs you know, people wish to reach their highest need—Self-actualization.

The world is not all that interested. Lying, cheating, broking promise, you just wonder why the lights are not turning green for you. That's why you bury yourselves in accomplishments, because with accomplishments, you believe that you could control things, you could squeeze in every last piece of happiness before you get sick and dye. Verily, the bigger accomplishments mean the more success and the more security. So, in this world, there are only two kinds of people: Winner and Loser, no so called good man or bad man. Just like Deng Xiaoping's (邓小平) famous aphorism: "No matter white cat or black cat, if the cat can catch the mouse, it is a good cat". Therefore, to search the endless accomplishments, you often feel confused and depressed.

Notwithstanding, a lot of thins are beyond your control due to your inability, unknown, and ever-changing environment. Only God can control everything. So, accepted what you are able to do and what are not able to do; accept the past as past, without denying it or discarding it; learn to forgive yourselves and to forgive others; don't assume that it's too late to get involved.

That is: Do the kind of things that come from your heart. When you do, you won't be envious, you wont' be longing for somebody else's things. On the contrary, you'll be overwhelmed with what comes back.

4.6 Security

Who is the owner of the earth?

In Mallow's hierarchy of needs, it is just in second level of basic need. However, it becomes a big concern for everyone even nation because in this global competitive environment out there full of insecurities. Who and what threatens to your security? Maybe policy change, technology advancement, better position or pay check, career promotion, or your competitors etc? It comes from greed or selfish. Everyone wish everything favors to him or for his own good, to get what he want, to do what he do? But resource is limited. Who deserves better social status, more power and money due to scared resources? We have only one earth. Who is the owner of the earth? Why there were so many countries being invaded or occupied? Why did World War I and World War II happen? When does World War III happen? As a country, now more and more nations pay attention to terrorism attack, that's why US have joined EU and other countries to fight for global terrorism due to security reason. From nation to company to individual, there are endless wars, disputes, conflicts, and arguments. So, can they happy? Can peace with them?

People are only mean when they're threatened. Their social status, face, love, money, human right etc, and when they get threatened, they start looking out only for themselves to protect them, not to lose them to keep the going. If serious, maybe they will use ruthless and despicable means to protect them. More power and more money mean more secure, even you can avoid the Law punishment in some circumstances because you can bribe the witness to false testimony due to

Law caring about evidence not truth. However, only God has definitely security.

4.7 Some surviving tips to live in China
4.71 Safety

What's the most concern when you station oversea? Your business performance, your career advancement or others, no, safety is the top priority. So, ask your family members never show off wealth or superiority, as humble as possible. Otherwise, safety is a problem there.

4.72 Shopping and going out

♦Do shopping in bigger supermarket, such as Wal-Mark, Carrefour, United Lihua etc

♦Do not buy food (raw or cooked) in small stall because the hygiene conditions maybe a problem.

♦Do not buy famous brand stuff in China because it is a fake with higher possibility and not deserve it.

♦Pay attention to your wallet, cell phone, and valuable belongings in train, bus, and the crowd street and ignore street beggars because you are foreigner and can be easily to their target.

♦Travel with your friend; if on your own, do not go to out-of-way.

4.73 Drink

If you have conflict or tough deal with your co-workers or business partners, No drunk for alcohol when drink with them. If so, maybe they have some tricks to ask you to sign something.

4.74 Be alert

Often check your car and house and office especially for blind spot: Is there any electronic device or spy camera or not?

4.75 Casual sex

"One night stand" is not a big deal in western countries; however for you in China, maybe it is a trap. They will take your picture and use it to blackmail you. So, check the room whether is equipped with spy camera especially for pin-hole camcorder because it is not easy to find; when you fall asleep, maybe they can use cell-phone with camera to take picture too. Therefore, "One hour stand" is better because you get pleasure without trouble. Another alternative is looking for hookers. Prostitutes are illegal, however out there everywhere in China. Check it out those hidden occasions such as "Beauty salon" or "Massage center" in small lanes or high class hotels. However, you are foreigners, the price maybe higher, therefore ask your friend for market price.

4.76 Look for a girl friend to marry

If you are lucky, you will get good one partner. But most of time it is not, you will get nightmare from her family, relatives and friends. So, as a friend Ok, marriage you need to consider more carefully especially her real intention.

Chapter5   Work

If you do not have enough money to do your own business in China, seizing a chance to work in China is another good option, because a spell in China will broaden your career horizon. After all, if you can succeed in running a factory or a trade office in China, it is an invaluable asset for you. However, working in China can be a frustrating experience. You have to learn to make adjustment to fit with the new environment. China is not going to change to suit you if you want to survive; you have to adapt it as soon as possible.

5.1 Human Resources

Every organization knows the importance of Human Resources as the final competition of their success. These Chinese CEOs appreciate the importance of talent people and organizations in strategic implementation, and they are playing a lot of attention to these issues. However, they have to address these issues based on their intuition and personal judgment. CEOs face tremendous challenges and opportunities of growth, globalization, and intensified competition for human capital. Partly due to impact of Chinese culture and partly due to their resource scarcity, many Chinese prefer to manage their firms based on trust, relationships, and shared entrepreneurial success, and market responsiveness.

5.11 Criteria

So, the most wanted talent's qualities for these CEOs are:
- Obedience
- Relationship
- Trust
- Finally, your competitive advantages, such as management, communication, computer skills, language etc

Due to underdeveloped management process and systems, reward and career development opportunities are largely tied to the personal judgment of these core managers, not to transport criteria and process. As a result, these opportunities reinforce the culture of personal relationship and loyalty within these organizations.

5.12 Energy Loss

The worst is "Energy Loss". Here we define energy as the percentage of a person's engagement at work, physically, mentally, spiritually, emotionally, and socially.

Many, if not most people, seldom bring their best effort to work; they seem to save them for evening and weekend. This is not to say that employees are not working; they are, and they are doing their jobs "good enough" (similar to quality perception), but in a global competitive business environment, good enough is not longer enough. Throughout the industrial era, the primary leadership approach to the problem of energy management was goal setting. The establishment of measure, the subsequent setting of goals, and then the management required for accomplishment, have formed the unexamined mantra of business leaders everywhere.

Here the difference is between choice and obligation. When we choose to do something, we have more energy for it. When we have to do something, our energy is likely to flag even if we set our own goals. That is: when we choose to do something, our energy level is likely higher; if we do a thing because we have to or because we feel obligated, our energy curve tends to flatten and even decline. So, if you are not within their network (at least at the beginning), plus no trust and respect, can you exert your 100% energy to your company?

Therefore, building a friendly and trust working environment and making job enjoyable are the critical factors to keep your staff to work by choice beyond goal setting. Let them work towards the performance of what it does, rather than just work another hour for X dollars.

5.13 "Vase" syndromes

Your are only a "Vase" or "Puppet"

A lot of Chinese enterprises especially for private have finished their first start and want to expand for the next move. However, due to economic globalization and modern management requirements, such as transparency, accountability, the previous business secret maybe does not work, therefore those Chinese owners hope to recruit professional manager to fulfill their dream. However, the biggest challenge faces for those owners is how to exert those professional talent whiles not conflict with different interest cliques in company especially for family members.

Most companies hire them on short term purpose. Either they can not afford to pay high salary on long term; or some companies hire oversea professionals for "going public" in oversea to gain global awareness and funding due to their unknown or for special purpose. For instance, in year 2005, Bank of China—Ha Erbin brunch hired Mr. Dong (Chinese American) as CEO of "Risk Management". After Bank of China went public in Oversea successfully, Mr. Dong resigned. Why, only the bank senior officer knew the real reasons. On the other hand, some companies hire professional especially those from oversea only as a "vase" or puppet to show owner's openness and global thinking or marketing purpose. Although they have senior position, such as Vice President or Deputy General Manager, most of time they do not have any real authority to perform their job or they are in air. That's the lose-lose situation for owners and professionals.

5.2 Organization

Select the right organization, keep your career soar. Only those organizations which have clear vision and mission statement, clear job authority and responsibility, potential for career advancement are the right one for your next career move. Take your time to check company background, such as website, brochure, customers or suppliers, investigate your boss leadership style, especially question this position is real or company wants you to replace someone or not? If "Yes" for the answer, do not join the company because you do not have a good end. Of course, it is not easy to get information due to limited resource, just try your best to get something to eliminate your risk. Why employer can check employee background whiles employee cannot? If you can't select the right organization or not fit to your boss leadership style, your career will be stopped. It is very difficult for you to turn from adversity.

Therefore, the best option is your home employers. If they want to hire you, they do the enough background checking and through serious consideration about your strength and weakness and think you are the most competitive candidate for the position. The most important is that you have the unique advantage there compared to local staff; the second one is joint-venture, it is a risky because you must deal with different culture and business background for another counterpart; the most risky one is typical Chinese company, such as state-own or family-oriented business. If you like challenge you can try. If you overcome the hurdle and succeed in surviving there about 3 years to get some accomplishments you will get abundant career advancement opportunities to soar in everywhere. If not, your career will be ruined due to bad-mouth of reference check.

5.3 Employment Agreement

If you decide to take the challenge to work in Chinese company, that's great, at least you are unique with bold and astute. Read the "Appointment letter" carefully, take about one week to consider the details terms and conditions, ask some questions:

●Is your authority and responsibility clearly defined?

●Is your terms and conditions, such as position, salary, annual leave and fringe benefits etc, understandable and indisputable?

●Is there any hidden terms and conditions? Possible causes you crazy.

●If problem arises, where to settle dispute? Most of time they hope to settle in local court. Had better not, Shanghai or Beijing seems better and fairer.

Please remember, salary is net monthly salary. Just forget about those "Stock Options" and "Profit-sharing" with bullshit, it is more practical to get your net salary, because anything can happen in any time; furthermore, salary is after tax, because personal income tax in China is very high (after converted to your currency), unless they are willing to pay for you.

After you join the company, do not make any compromise with your agreement. If you give in one time, your trouble there, you lose your bargaining power for the next time.

5.4 Salary

It is another embarrassing situation which causes resenting by local staff that you must face. In envelope, it is confidential, but do not know, finally all staff knows your salary. It seems they offer you very attractive package because company wants to globalization. However, it is only market price converted to your currency.

Because your salary is 10-20 times higher than your local staff, even your boss. What they expect from you? You are superman!! But actually you are not. What you have just western management style for different expertise in different

70

areas, such as marketing, operations, or finance. Furthermore, a company success is a team-work. You can not perform the entire job in your own. For example, your company can not delivery product on time, or have some quality defects. Those problems can happen in every stage or process. Maybe demand forecast, capacity planning, purchasing, manufacturing process, or quality control. So, when something happens, ask you to solve immediately. Can you, superman? Because you have so high salary, so you should have magic.

5.5 Your Family

Everyday, your mind is occupied with problems, troubles and challenges. Meeting with people, negotiating deal, solving problems, coordinating conflict, gaining extra insights into the society with which you must now cope, things are much tougher for the wives left to spend the day in an apartment or, even worse, in the confines of a hotel room; the more stifling is the children. Imagine yourself a western teenager in China. Back home, life would be an endless round of school, parties, picnics, sports events, fashions, dating, overnight stay with friends, trips to the countryside, movie-going, hobbies and all the other joys of growing up and exploring life. In China, life is much more restricted. There are far fewer opportunities for enjoying the best years of your life.

So, when accepting overseas posting in China, do not just think about leaping at the opportunity, but weight things up, what's that mean for your family? How long you will stay there? If you are single, you can ignore those issues. If you have family, consider: your family wants to go with you or separate? Is there any suitable school for your child's education? If separate, ask questions: can your marriage survive with such lengthy separation?

5.6 Team

Build your own team

A team is an organization with its own dynamics, qualities and conventions. In every team, there are a variety of people all pushing and shoving in different directions and with unequal force. A team does not pull together well when each individual member focuses on their target---be that just getting to the end of the day. If you are the team manager: Build your own team—the first step. If you can not recruit all the team members, at least you can select them as your team members who you can trust to work in your team or unit. As a result, networks are created within a larger network.

Getting your team to soar takes courage, grit, determination and an overwhelming passion. You can not achieve something with your single-handed; you need your team members to support. So, trusting them, training them, getting them the best resource, supporting them, finally you make your team better than you.

Image you are foreigner, what's your foundation there—zero, how can you compete with local staff. If you can not build your own team and network, the higher possibility that you are stabbed in the back.

5.7 Privacy

Your everything maybe under surveillance

It is taken for grand in western society because it is basic need for personal dignity and is strictly protected by law. However, in China, most people do not have such concept.

Privacy, what's that? For what? Another phenomenon is that technology advancement provides the hotbed for those people with evil desire to intrude your privacy. Spy camera, electronic recorder, phone monitoring device, spy software, spy e-mail, computer decoding system, etc provide hidden monitoring without any authorization. So, sometime people just argue: technology is a good thing or a bad thing? Well, if it is used to improve quality of life, it is a good thing. However, if it is misused by third party to monitor something without authorization, it is a bad thing.

The Internet is a daunting and transparent place. Because all software programs contain bugs and holes that can compromise the security of the computers it is running on. Malicious individuals on the Internet can attack your computer and compromise your data. Therefore plan a 'safe and security' strategy to protect your computer activity.

Everyone has his own privacy or secret and should be protected by law. No privacy, no trust, no integrity, and no respect.

It is dilemma for Chinese employers especially for family-oriented companies. They want to hire you, ask you to make contribution for their growth. However, they worry about your hostile taking over or playing tricks. How to avoid that? Most of them do not know how to access your credential fully and simply hire you by gut-feeling. What they think practical is to test you after employment. If they test you through caring, observation, and communication, it is acceptable for every professional. However, they take the quick, easy and despicable way to "surveillance": your daily phone conversation, your activities at home, your computer activities, your e-mail transaction etc. And they assume you do not know what they do because they monitor secretly or hidden. Really? Unless you are an idiot. Are you happy with that? Since no trust, no respect, how to ask you to contribute your talent. Finally result is lose-lose for both parties.

5.8 Some surviving tips in Chinese workplace

5.81 Privacy

If you do care your personal privacy, follow those steps as follows, maybe it is helpful.

5.811 Your computer

● Buy anti-spy software to protect your every e-mail transaction, internet browsing, computer activity and update your software in time. It is the best way.

●Change the log-on mode with user only (no other options to log-on)

●Set security to high in Internet option while turn on window fireball in control panel if you want to protect your computer activity; In addition, for special document, add password to protect it.

●Go to local "Internet cafe" or at home to browse your private interested topic, do not do it in your company.

●Change your password often for your e-mail account. Had better not easy to guess your password.

5.812 Telephone

Prepare two cell-phones; one for company, the other is for you. Only give your personal number to whom you trust. It is possible that your company want to monitor your phone conversation due to no trust.

5.813 Accommodation

If possible, rent the apartment yourself. If your company arranges for you, sounds very good. But it is possible you are monitored by some devices

5.82Your family

Take your wife and child with you on an exploratory trip, talk to as many foreigners as possible and discuss shopping, schools, entertainment and other aspects of life in your home city, if they like it, there you go.

5.83 Join the Club or Community

Every newcomer faces in China had been met and overcome by people already living there. They have been in your boat—confused, perplexed, bewildered, irritated by the unexplainable—and are pleased to soothe your fears and explain the form. If you doubt, ask.

5.84 Office

●Be active, not passive

Plan your career goal more realistic, predict the consequences as more as possible, and prepare for the worst situation, because you are new for the environment. Otherwise, if something happens to you, you will get lost.

●Do not bad mouth your boss

If you can not find anything good to say, then say nothing. Because it is your choice to work for him, you have to stick with him, live with him, support with him—otherwise, you get mad. If you can not tolerate his leadership and behavior anymore, go look some other place.

●Do not show off your shrewd in front of your boss

Even you are smart; never show it in front of your boss in every circumstance, such as office meeting, site, or entertainment. First, it can keep his face, because he is the owner of the company; second he will feel secure. If he knows you are clearer than he, you will not have a good end.

●Do not know too much

Perform your job in your scope. Knowing too much is not a good thing especially for company shady business deals or your boss dirty behaviors. If you want to show off because you know everything you will not have a good end.

●Do not offend your boss' relatives

Because they are family tie with deep relationship, loyalty and trust, on the other hand, maybe boss ask them to monitor you actively as mole. So, even you do not mean to offend them, they bad mouth about you to boss, your all effort will be ruined. Because you are new for the boss, your credibility and trust under test.

●Adapt your style to the environment

You are unique and have special skills required by the company, however, you work in different environment, study and observe your environment, your team member, and your department staff, be sensitive to them and work with them. Adapt your management style accordingly without change your skin and personality. For example, why Coke Cola has more than 100 tastes because it wants to accommodate to different country's taste, the same as Chinese food in western, it is modified to fit your taste.

●Fight for your team

Your accomplishment relies not only on your ability but also your team member's effort. So, build your great team and fight for your team to deliver desirable result.

●Play politics?

In western, most managers avoid to play politics in company. If you perform job well, everything will be OK. However, it is not the case in typical Chinese company. There are different interest-groups, so, what group you will stand for? Maybe none, if none, no one will support you.

Intimidating people, getting things done by lying or using other despicable means, being sly, that's politics. Every group wants to secure its interest, you work there, no choice to be yourself or true to others. So, observe and weigh, then decide to join which group as your backer to secure your position. But it is still risky because things can change. Maybe the group you join finally lose. Or if there is interest conflict, your boss will sacrifice you to protect his interest. As a result, you lose your job.

●Tell truth?

Everyone likes straight and deserves to know the truth. But in this turbulent and competitive environment, people lying, cheating, or dirty dealing for their purpose in special occasions. It is a dilemma for you to tell truth in the occasion. Keep silence, if you can not satisfy your boss, let it be. You will probably lose job if serious, because the price of remaining clean, honest and decent is very high indeed.

●Keep promise

Always keeping promise for your team or staff if you promise something, because keeping promise means keeping your face. Try your best to do it. If you can not do it due to force majeure, amend it and explain to them. You will earn appreciation, loyalty and respect.

●Control your mood

To some extend, EQ is more important than IQ. Because Chinese are indirect and hidden, you need more times to understand what's the situation and going on then you can make decision. Otherwise the thing will get worse.

●Be patient

Be patient to your boss, your underlings, your customers, and suppliers. Spend more time with them; observe what they say and what they act, especially for face reading, body language and subtle remarks? Because Chinese are indirect and hidden, they have different facets and behaviors in different situations. So, you often confuse and do not know how to tell when is true or false, when "Yes" means "Yes", when means "No"? Take your spare time to build relationship with them. The more time you spend, the more real feeling they can tell.

Chapter6   Case

Most authors keen on presenting notable successes to encourage readers. However, here I list six unforgettable mistake cases about marriage, business partner and office politics. After you read, seek what lessons can you learn? What key factors brought monumental mistake? Through such evaluations and studies, you may learn to improve "Batting average" in the intriguing, ever-challenging art of decision making.

"50 lessons from the boardroom" is great; however, these cases are not practical in Chinese cultural and business environment.

6.1 Case 1

> **Happy families are all alike;
> every unhappy is unhappy in its own way**

"Happy families are all alike; every unhappy family is unhappy in its own way". Everyone knows the epigraph to Anna Karenina. However, the following case maybe unhappy in its own way.

Mr. David knew Ms. Linda in 1995 through his alumni's introduction when back to home China and understood that Linda wished to transferred to provincial capital city through her marriage but unsuccessful. Davis did not care about it if Linda married him sincerely because he thought there was not true love in the world. Staying together two days, both had an initial good impression each other. What moved David was: when David told Linda that he went to Singapore only 6 months, the financial situation was not so strong compared to native Singaporean, Linda said "It is fine, for quality of life, we can fight for it because we are smart." So, David agreed for further connection through writing. After courtship of six months, they married in China. David applied "Permanent Resident" for Linda and the application was approved within another six month.

To help Linda to get foothold in Singapore, David ask Linda to attend computer and English courses in China during green card application, however, she did not care about it. So, when Linda came to Singapore, it was a real problem for her to get the job because she lacked of basic computer and language skills. Fortunately David was an employment agent and got the job for her. But David told Linda: if you want good career prospect you had better master more skills. So, David helped her to study English and computer at home, taught her office skill, and found the relative course for her in Singapore to upgrade her. After another six months, David found another job for Linda with better position and pay and decided to have a baby. David's reason was: now we bought our own flat, both had a good job and some saving; moreover, we were not young (David was 35, Linda was 30 at the time), if we wanted to have a health and clever baby, it was time. But Linda denied with her worries: we were still struggle for life; it was not the right time to have a kid. So, David worked harder to get more customers for bigger pay check. At the same time, Linda asked David to find job for her sister and apply social visit for her mother. Although it was not easy, David tried his best to help and finally succeeded.

After another year, Linda thought that she could stand her foot in Singapore firmly and got what she wanted. Her attitude toward David was totally different from before. She found any chance to quarrel with David. Below was dialogue about the same issue for kid.

"OK, if you want to have a kid, pays me S$100,000.00 to my saving account, and has a successful career within 3 years, plus condo and car, then I will consider. Only you can satisfy for those conditions them I will feel security because after I have a baby, I will lose my job and become ugly."

"Oh, my God. First, kid is our kid, not my kid. If you want kid to trade in, it is no point for us. Second, those material things, we can strive to it, but it needs time. Third, if women over 30, it is difficult to have a kid, even have maybe it is not a clever one, now you are over 31. Forth, for security, we can work together to overcome every hardship if have. Only God has definitely security."

"You treat me as a tool to have kid, no, I am not the one. Only we have a stable love relationship, then we can have". 'Why you marry me?"

"I want to breach poverty and leave underdeveloped mountain area however I paid the price of marriage. Why I came to Singapore, of course for quality of life and more opportunity? Like my look and clever head, I should have richer man not like you."

"Ok, go ahead, let's break up".

Since David saw through Linda's real intention to marry him, he decided to divorce with Linda and went to US for further study to forget this unhappy marriage. But his family disagreed, because divorce was not a good thing for Chinese and his friends persuaded him to forgive and tolerate each other. At the time, Linda thought she did not find a suitable rich man yet, why no wait and see if David has a good future, just put up with him to escape moral censure. So, David gave her another chance and thought this was time to test their marriage for two years separation.

After David got his MBA degree, he went to China to explore his career horizon due to perceived China huge opportunities and thought maybe this was the quick way to succeed his career to satisfy her wife's expectations to maintain the marriage upon Linda's approval. So, his position leaped from Chief Operations Officer to General Manager and changed three employers within three years. However, when David wanted to soar for another better position he failed because the owner found David changed so many jobs in short period and suspected his loyalty.

When man fails in career what he wants is family support and encourage. However, Linda did not do that because she did not love him at all. So, she asked David to petition in Family Court because only this she can get the alimony. David felt so sad that after ten years marriage he had nothing and decided to divorce with Linda. However, Linda wanted David to pay her "Youth Loss" because David petitioned first. David denied with this nonsense saying. Linda could not get what she want, this wicked lady sued David for committing "Family violence" through "telephone conversation". The Family Court in Singapore denied issue "Personal protection order" for Linda due to her inconsistency evidence on September 15, 2006. After more than one year's contesting, they finally divorced on Jan, 10, 2007 in Singapore however Linda still asked David to pay her the alimony even one dollar per month.

Questions 1: At the beginning when David knew Linda's conditional marriage, why he did not care? Did he make the first mistake?
Questions 2: When David got Linda's intention to marry him, why he did not divorce for the face of his family, friends and himself? Did he make the second mistake?
Questions 3: To satisfy his wife expectations, David rushed to China for his career jump and did not plan his career goal carefully? Did he make the third mistake?
Questions 4: What lessons can you learn from this case?

6.2 Case 2

Turn their tricks against them

将计就计

Robert got the job offer— "Operation Director Assistant" in Guangdong in year 2001 on a Hong Kong based machinery assembly company after he earned his MBA degree. Only after he joined the company two months then he knew that there were some unfavorable opinions from 'Board of Director" against his boss—Mr. Chris who was a smart and practical man especially skilled in conjecturing Owner's psychology. Although his education was below O level, he got promotion from workshop apprentice to Operation Director within 10 years. However, as a Director, the job duties are different from workshop. Most of time concerned about managing the people and strategic decision-making, his style was the same as workshop level and he was not willing to upgrade himself. So, some shareholders hoped to recruit one who has modern management concept, knowledgeable, and experience to replace him. They did not know when they could get the one and did not let Chris to know their purpose due to normal operation. They persuade Chris to recruit assistant because he was busy with the whole plant operation as a reason.

At the beginning, Chris was reluctant to do it because he could handle the normal operation. As times going, Chris felt pressure about this issue because they raised it three times and knew their intention, and decided to turn their trick against them. So, Chris recruited Robert from "Job Fair" and hoped Robert could join his clique to secure his position because Robert's everything was in his hand.

After Robert knew the situation, he felt upset. If he wanted to survive in the company, he must please his boss and get trust and support from him. However, after another three months, he found there was a big different leadership style with his boss and him. The dilemma was: Robert must outperform with his boss, but under his boss. Can he do that without any support from the boss of his boss? Finally he left the company about five months.

Questions 1: Must Robert investigate the company background and their real intention to recruit this position prior to his employment? Is it easy for a foreigner to do so? Did Robert make the first mistake?

Questions 2: Was Robert impatient to accommodate his style to fit Chris to survive or since there was much different style just switch? Did Robert make the second mistake?

Questions 3: How did Robert outperform with Chris without any support or how to get support from other shareholders because he had zero foundation there?

Questions 4: What lessons can you learn from this case?

6.3 Case 3

Jie dao sha ren 借刀杀人

Jie dao sha ren 借刀杀人

Mr. Fisher, Mr. Douglas, and Mr. Circle were "Three "Represents" in one "Electrical Group". The Croup succeeded previously due to central planned economy, (The government asked customers to buy products form the group) however, as market economy merged to command economy, there was no more such advantage for the group. Because they were satisfied with their accomplishments and slow to response to market, so the group sales dropped down dramatically. The more serious was: three representatives could not reach the agreement for group strategy adjustment toward the market and always fought each other. So, Fisher applied "Jie dao sha ren" (借刀杀人) (making use of another persons to remove his barrier) trick and decided to recruit senior management staff from Hong Kong to replace all the core managers. So, when Hongkongers got there, there were some changes there: one Hongkonger was President, Fisher as Vice President, Circle as GM, Douglas was transferred to as "Region sales manager", CFO and HR manager changed also. But things were not going smooth as Fisher imagined. Finally those Hongkongers left with regret. The failure reasons were: First, Fisher did not get any agreement with Douglas and Circle to hire Hongkongers, how to ask their support? Second, everyone needs security. If something threatens to them, they start looking out only for themselves to protect them, nothing different with Douglas, Lucy and Circle. Third, change. Everyone resists changing because of unknown, inability, or fear. So, to facilitate this strategic decision, management must plan carefully; analyze the cost/benefit of change, train the staff, and then change gradually to smooth the process successful. However, Fisher underestimated the difficulty of change.

Forth, the advantage of Hongkongers is that they are familiar with western business/management style, however they are not superman. They must get enough support to do something. Furthermore, two much salary gap is another problem for them.

Fifth, the group did not evaluate the candidates and the group situation. No resume screening, background, criminal and credit checking because there was not such H.R recruitment procedure before.

After first mistake, Fisher did not give up and tried second time. This time he was more carefully to select candidate and fortunately recruited only one—Tim who got his MBA degree from US with native Chinese. Below was dialogue about Tim and Fisher at Career Expo in Hong Kong.

"Why your company wants to recruit foreigner?"

"Our company wants to globalization to sustain competitiveness. What we want are those who have western management style and experience plus understanding insightful Chinese culture. You are the one."

"You recruited Hongkongers six months ago, did you satisfy with their performance."

"Yes."

Tim was admired by Fisher's ability to create economic miracle in a small northern poor city and thought since this was the second time to recruit foreigners the company must have great expansion, so, finally he decided to join the company as COO in year 2002. However, when Tim joined the Group, the Group assigned him the different position from COO to "Production coordinator", but salary kept unchanged. Tim was angry with that and prepared to pack bag to go home. However, Fisher persuaded him to stay.

"Perform yourself, if you are really capable, you will win finally. From base is good for you because you can understand what's going on there and get hand on experience. Even you keep the same position, but if you can not pass the probation, you are still to leave".

Tim agreed without choice. He went to workshop, operated machine, handle different problems and quality defects on site, communicated with staff. Finally he won respect from all levels and got promotion from "Production coordinator" to "Production Manager", then COO within fourth Months.

Tim's quick promotion, plus first time political movement, Dogalas thought it was a threat to him and organized the meeting of BOD in year end to re-position the key staff with his wife Lucy. Tim and other key staff talked to Fisher. Since BOD agreed to promote someone just one month, why you wanted to change so quickly? If so, how to stabilize key staff and other staff emotion? However, the group had year end meeting of BOD and re-arrange the position for core managers. Finally, Fisher as President, Circle as GM of old factory, the biggest winner was Douglas, as GM, and his wife, Lucy as "Chief Administration Officer", CFO was also under his clique. Tim's position was the same, but was in air just like a "Vase".

Tim tried his best to fight for his real position and hope to get support from Fisher. However, it was unsuccessful. He felt perplexed and wanted to figure out: Why Fisher (biggest shareholder) was President and could not make some critical decision such as H.R? Finally he knew that previously there were some deals with Fisher and Douglas and Lucy when company transited from state-own company to share holding group and built the industrial park.

Tim left the group about nine months, other foreigners left too.

Key staff position adjustment as follows:

Fisher: President—Vice President (President to Hongkonger)—President again;
Douglas: Fisher's driver—GM of Industrial Park—Region Sales Manager—GM of Group; Lucy: CFO—Chief Administration Officer, Dogalas' wife, Fisher's cousin;
Circle: GM of Group—GM of Old Factory;
Tim: Production Coordinator—Production Manager—COO (Chief Operations Officer)
Note: The group has two physical locations: one in old factory, another in industrial park

Question 1: Was Tim to naïve to trust Fisher that Fisher was satisfied with Hongkongers' performance in first recruitment? Did he make the first mistake to join the group?
Question 2: Should Tim deny the Fisher's different arrangement when Tim joined the group? Did he make the second mistake?
Question 3: At the beginning, Tim did not want to play 'Office Politics', however, he could not get any support from Fisher, Douglas and Circle. When he joined the group, he knew that there was stronger power in Douglas' clique, must he switch to Douglas but it was Fisher who recruited him? Did he make the third mistake to join Fisher clique?
Question 4: How to fight Tim's real authority to perform his job well?
Question 5: What lessons can you learn from this case?

6.4 Case 4

Mr. King was a nice and kind gentleman and running his 'Steel Pipe Mill' more than 20 years. Because his hard working and persistence, King has finished his start mill operation from 6 people in year 1982 to more than 1000 staff in year 2003. Now King wants to expand his company and build his own product brand on a global base due to China joined WTO. Currently, the most important issue is how to recruit loyal and competent professional to fulfill his dream. Mark, followed him about 16 years, was practical and loyal, but short of modern management and technical expertise, workshop manager was his career ceiling; Tom, his nephew, the most trust one, was smart, but narrow-minded. So, he decided to go to Shanghai to recruit his desirable candidate secretly.

He got the candidate Mr. John and asked him to join the company as "GM" after Chinese New Year (2004). When John joined the company, King told John to handle a big capital investment project instead of GM because he was the most suitable one to be in charge. John was not happy with his arrangement but accepted this challenging and exciting project because it concerned about "Technical consultation", "Contract negotiation", "Production line import", 'Factory building and layout" etc. However, when this project team went to Germany to site visit and technical consultation, Mark and Bill objected John to join them to visit due to their potential position security and asked King to transfer John to "Import &Export" department. The problem was that King agreed their suggestion and transferred John to "Import &Export" department after three months.
John accepted King's arrangement and transferred to "Import &Export" department. The trouble was there because Tom was in charge of Marketing and sales department and obviously as GM next year. So, why his uncle arranged another competitor to him? No, he did not want to have

another barrier for his career advancement. Tom used trust and loyalty to warn King: "How do you know his intention to join our company? John seems shrewd, it is higher risky to get all our customers and vendors as his own good?"

King accepted Tom's advice and monitored John hidden and secretly, including phone conversation, e-mail transaction, computer activity, and others to test his loyalty and trust. At the beginning, John was not aware of it. As time going, he felt strange: why they could know his feeling and thought? He felt angry and talk to them hidden: please respect my privacy. But they did not care about it and monitor more hidden. After that, John had not any motivation to contribute his valuable ideas to the company.

After another four months, Tom thought the "Import &Export" department was running better than before and John was not used for him any more. He asked King to transfer John to Project team against. This time John denied the arrangement and finally left company in ten months.

Key staff position:
Mr. King: Owner, CEO; Mr. Tom, Executive Deputy GM, Mr. King's nephew;
Mr. Mark: GM; Mr. Bill: Chief Engineer, 66 years old
John: Deputy GM

Question 1: Did John make first mistake to accept King's different arrangement when joined?
Question 2: Since King arranged John to project team, why he agreed Mark and Bill's suggestion not to let John to visit Germany in this key project stage? Did John make the second mistake to give in to King?
Question 3: Why King transferred John to Project team again after John stayed in "Import &Export" department forth months? Did John make the third mistake to deny the arrangement?

Question 4: How to show your loyalty to Owner and gain trust from him?

Question 5: What lessons you can learn from this case?

6.5 Case 5

Mr. George had acquired a local state-own automotive component manufacturing plant 10 years ago and hopes to have second start for his business expanding. The 60% of the company products was exported to EU and US. Due to short of export talent, the company exported the products through export agent. George wished to recruit key staff to help him to set up an export department whiles streamline internal operation system to meet the customer's comprehensive expectations for TS16949. That's why George recruited Ken as his assistant and his son's mentor in Oct, 2004. The biggest challenge for Ken was not to smooth internal operations, but how to balance George's family members. Because this company was located in a small town, his family questions not only the integrity and loyalty of Ken, but also the motive of Ken to join the company. So, when Ken joined the company, his family members were reluctant to accept him and let him in airs. The more serious was: they monitor Ken's every activity including phone conversation, e-mail transaction, computer activity, and others. Ken was not happy with that and left the company within one month.

George felt sorry for that and thought it was not easy to get a capable staff like Ken who was willing to work in a small town. He apologized sincerely and invited Ken back to the company and promised with following conditions:

●No privacy intrusion
●The company follows his instructions and extends their full support
●All staff must co-operate with him

So, Ken went back to company, got data from relative departments, had a detail business and operation plan to reform the company to reach the short term and lone term goals. He paid special attention to staff training and development because only qualified staff can produce quality products. However, George's wife disagreed with the plan and suspected that "If Ken controls everything; it is not far for him to hostile take over". Actually George had the same worry. So, they continued monitor Ken, and most of time Ken socialized with his family members and George, as a result, Ken left the company after another three months.

Mr. George: Owner, MD; George's son: GM; George's wife: CFO;
George's daughter: Purchasing Manager; George's son-in-law: H.R Manager;
George's brother-in-law: Production Manager; George's brother: Engineering Manager; Lee: Deputy GM, 66 years old; Ken: Executive Deputy GM, MD Assistant, George Son's mentor

Questions 1: Should Ken forgive George and go back to the company after George invited him back? What mistake Ken make?
Questions 2: Could George keep his promises to Ken in such family-oriented business environment?
Questions 3: How to meet George's expectations and not to offense his family members?
Questions 4: What lessons can you learn from this case?

6.6 Case 6

Pat and Jacky (Taiwanese) knew each other when Pat worked as "Operations Director" in one Electrical Company, and Jacky as on site auditor for potential order. As time going, Jacky realized that Pat was honest, capable, and good financial status but eager to his own career. Catching Pat's weakness, Jacky encouraged Pat to resign and open a new company with him as a new big order from Italy was coming soon. Pat was not happy to work there due to 'Office Politics' and thought this was a good chance for him; another reason was that Jacky seemed loyal to friend. So, Pat went with Jacky to Guangdong to wait and prepare for the order in year 2003.

After two months in Guangdong, Jacky's boss—Steven visited them two times and told them to sourcing for testing instruments and parts. So, they got all the sourcing and parts and waited for it. However, another month passed by, nothing about the order. Pat got angry and asked Jacky the reason. Jacky told Pat that he was cheated by Steven too because he benefited nothing and wasted his time. "But never mind, I have another business. My 70% of customers have shifted from Taiwan to China, therefore, I will try my best to get them back in China, and I already have a good supplier for "Plastic injection parts and molding", your job just to on site audit, capacity planning and schedule shipping. Don't worry, you help me a lot, you would get rewards".

So, Pat trusted Jacky one more time and sometimes went to Karaoke club with Jacky to entertain his clients or friends to build relationship. Actually Pat was not used to such occasions but for business prospect he had no choice. After another three months, Jacky thought that everything was OK for him and it was time to kick Pat out, because he knew Pat's another weakness—impatience. He just continued to ask Pat go to Karaoke club every night and be patience for the order because it was difficult to anticipate when the order would come in. After Pat saw through Jacky, Pat terminated their cooperation.

Questions 1: Did Pat make first mistake just by Jacky's pretence loyalty to join him?

Questions 2: Select good partner as your business success is very important. What are important factors to be considered as a good business partner, personal integrity, financial situation, or expertise? How to get the information across the country?

Question 3: Most people lose by petty gain. Should Pat verify and wait for the real order coming then join Jacky? How to verify the order?

Question 4: What lessons can you learn from this case?

NOT THE END

1. After you read, maybe you will feel that life in China is not easy. It is! In west, most people enjoy life, however in China most people struggle for life. Stress for better quality life, better social status, more power, more money, maybe the harder is better terms than others. So, the game is endless. Currently, the three big mountains oppressed for vast majority Chinese are: employment, housing, and public order. People live with caution, what to say and how to do is a matter, even a small matter. As a result, you are a foreigner: **Think before you leap.**

In west most people enjoy life;
however in China most people struggle for life

2. China has 32 markets. Hence, if you want to invest in one province, do research thoroughly. Because every province has its own market and sub-culture, no one single market in China. They impose their own barriers and restrictions to protect their own provincial enterprise. The result is economic waste, inefficiency and duplication as a nation.

3. Chinese people do desire to change to improve their culture and business environment for the better, especially for younger generations. People are bored of life with mask. However, if there is any interest conflict with the change that is the serious matter for them.

Now, not only the Chinese people but also the West people appreciate "**Simplicity**" life in countryside or small village in old China. They hope no-distortion four qualities of Rujiao "Ren, Yi, Dao, De". I do wish China can become a superpower nation like in Tang Dynasty. When?

4. Due to technology advancement, communication improvement, cheap air-ticket and travel promotion, now

people in the world is becoming more and more alike. Internet, Pub, Multimedia, Drug, Aids, Game, even Gay and Lesbian are all over the China. Selfish, greed, hypocrisy, deception, fraud, corruption, violence, and so on are not only in China, they are global phenomenon.

If we see each other as more alike, we might be very eager to join in one big human family in this world, and to care about that family the way we care about our own.

Appendix 1

Chinese Dynasties

Xia	—3000 BC to 1562 BC
Shang	—1562 BC to 1066 BC
Zhou	—1066 BC to 221 BC
Qin	—221 BC to 206 BC
Han	—206 BC to AD 220
The Three Kingdoms	—220 to 265
Jin	—265 to 420
Southern and Northern Dynasties	—420 to 581
Sui	—581 to 618
Tang	—618 to 907
Five Dynasties & Ten Kingdoms	—907 to 960
Song	—960 to 1271
Yuan	—1271 to 1368
Ming	—1368 to 1644
Qing	—1644 to 1911
Republic of China	—1911 to 1949
People's Republic of China	—1949

Thick Black School

厚 黑 学

Author, Li Zongwu (1879-1944)born in Zigong, Sichuan, worked for Minister of Education and positioned as Principle of high school, MP of Provincial and Deputy-Director of Education department of Sichuan Province. He was intelligent and upright and wished to be hero since childhood. Therefore he studied <Four Books>, <Five Classics>, searched Confucius and Menzi for nothing, then initiated and developed his own life philosophy and wrote the book <Thick Black School>. It criticized and exposed mercilessly to the Chinese autocratic system hypocrisy, feudal ethics, social darkness and official corruption and has become a rare national sensation masterpieces and the best seller from 1980's in Taiwan, Hong Kong and Japan. Although it is called "Shameless books" by someone, its techniques and tactics for human relationship work definitely in this global complex and competitive environment, big issue such as politics, economy, military and academic etc to routine such as social occasions, business negotiation, business deal, office politics, personal conflict, cultural clash and so forth in Chinese culture and business environment. If you apply adequately it is amazing.

In essence, the book has ***three steps, nine codes and eighty-one rules*** as follows. Although I do not agree some opinions of this book, most of them work not only in east but also in west.

The first step: Thick as wall, black as coal

At the beginning, the cheek as thin likes a piece of paper, then from inch to feet finally as thick as wall. The original color of the heart likes milk, then to blue, finally as black as coal. To this realm, it can only be described as its initial effort because: although the wall is thick it may be destroyed with bombers; the coal is black, it is dirty and disgusting, nobody wants to get close to it.

The second step: thick and hard, black and shine

The people who is insight in thick is unbeatable even you try to attack him, such as Liu Bei. Cao Cao can do nothing to him. The people who is profound in black likes the signboard of paint-fade, the more back the more buyers, such as Cao Cao who was the famous heartless. If you can get to second step, it is the big difference with first step but you still have signs with visible and color. Therefore, we can see through Cao Cao at the first meet even he was a hero.

The third step: thick but invisible, black but colorless

Most people think, although 'thick and black' has amazing result, it is not easy to achieve, maybe only for saint. Someone just wonder: "Is it so profound?" I say:" Yes, Confucian moderate turned to 'wushengwuxi' before terminated; Buddhist turned to 'no Bodhi tree ming jin fei tai' to fruition; moreover 'thick black school' is mysterious, if you want to accomplish the goal you must be 'invisible and colorless'".

李宗吾（1879-1944），四川自贡人，长期从事教育工作，历任中学校长、省议员、省长署教育厅副厅长等职。为人正直，聪颖机智，从小就希望成为英雄，因此，读《四书》、《五经》，研究孔孟之道，但一无所获。目睹人间冷暖，看透宦海浮沉，研究出自己一套完整的人生哲学，愤世写出"厚黑学"。作者对中国专制制度下虚伪的封建伦理和圣贤进行了无情的揭露和批判。其书从八十年代以来在台湾、香港及日本成为最畅销的书本。其侧重在中国文化心理下的为人处事指导，详细分析了各种为人技巧和处世经验，对当下处于激烈竞争社会现实环境的人去适应复杂多变的人际关系和心态调整有一定的参考价值，从大到政治、经济、军事及教育等，小到平常的社交、商务谈判、合同签约等都很有效，若应用得当，会产生神奇的作用。

概括起来，《厚黑学》有三个步骤、九个法则及八十一个准则。

其三步骤如下：

第一步：厚如城墙，黑如煤炭。

起初的脸皮，好像一张纸，由分而寸、由尺而丈，就厚如城墙了。最初心的颜色，作乳白状，由乳色而炭色，而青兰色，进而就黑如煤炭了。到了这个境界，只能算初步功夫；因为城墙虽厚，轰以大炮，还是有攻破的可能；煤炭虽黑，但颜色令人讨厌，众人都不愿接近它。所以只是初步的功夫。

第二步：厚而硬，黑而亮

深于厚学的人，任你如何功打，他一点不动，刘备就是这类人，连曹操都拿他没办法。深于黑学的人，如退光漆招牌，越是黑，买主越多，曹操就是这类人，他是著名的黑心子。能够到第二步，固然同第一步有天渊之别，但还露迹象，有形有色，所以曹操的本事，我们一眼就看出来了。

第三步：厚而无形，黑而无色

至厚至黑，天上后事，皆以为不厚不黑，这个境界，很难达到，只好在古天大圣大贤中去寻求，有人问"这种学问哪有这样精深？"我说："儒家的中庸，要讲到'无声无息'方能终止；学佛的人，要讲到'菩提无树，明镜非台'才算正果；何况厚黑是千古不传之秘，当然要做到'无形无色'才算止境"。

Code 1:
Cater to one's pleasure to win one's heart
投其所好操人心

Rule 1:
Flatter sincerely to build good talking environment
捧之有道，营造气氛

《宗吾真言》人都有觅求同类或知音的倾向，只要能使对方将你纳入知音的行列，你就有了良好的交流气氛。为此，说话初始阶段必须小心谨慎，有的放矢、投其所好，而不能惹人反感、叫人生厌。

《宗吾真言》为了营造良好的谈话气氛，一定要善于做一个善解人意的好听众。有些人喜欢唠叨个没完，一遍遍地诉苦，或没完没了地恭维，以为这样就能博得对方的好感，殊不知过犹不及，效果将会适的其反。

\<Zongwu's word\> Human inclines to seek confidant. If you can get it, then you have a good talking environment. Therefore, mind your word at the beginning, cater to his pleasure, not caused disguise or boring.

\<Zongwu's word\> To build a good talking environment you must act as a good and understanding listener. Someone thinks to win favor through nagging, complaint, or flattering, but it is not.

Rule 2:
Praise from your heart
真心赞美, 诚心恭维

《宗吾真言》不要吝啬自己的称赞，把它当成一种无本的投资，时间长了必然会得到回报。对别人来说，称赞是欣赏，是感谢，是对别人表示敬意，但对你来说只要厚着脸皮就能做出来。

《宗吾真言》吹捧不留痕迹； 恭维不致反感。

《宗吾真言》要达到真心赞美，诚心恭维，最要紧的是还是热诚。因此，每当你吹捧别人时，不可仅从大处着眼，有时还要从小处发挥。

\<Zongwu's word\> Praise someone frequently as a priceless investment, you will get reward in long-term. For others, praise is appreciation, thank and respect, but you can do it just thick-skin.

\<Zongwu's word\>Flatter sincerely, praise adequately.

\<Zongwu's word\>The key to praise or flattering is your passion. Therefore, you can flatter someone in every occasion, not only big issues, but also small matters.

Rule 3:
To be kind and gengle
you can get sizable reward
人好水甜, 花好月圆

《宗吾真言》说话看"火候",这里的火候是指时机，是说双方在能谈得开、说的拢的时候，对方愿意接受的时候。可是，火候不仅要看要等，还要善于创造和把握。

\<Zongwu's word\>Seize the good opportunity to talk, then you can get desirable result. Here opportunity means both sides have same topic, interest or the counterpart is willing to accept. However, you can wait for the opportunity, most of time you can create or crab it.

Rule 4:
Act likes celebrity,talk likes negotiator
演技高明，言语得体

《宗吾真言》谦恭有礼在说话中，首先表现在打招呼上。和别人打交道，总是以称呼开头，它好像是一个见面礼，又好像是进入社交大门的通行证。称呼得体，可使对方感到亲切，交谈便有了基础。以免引起对方的不快或愤怒，双方陷入尴尬境地。

《宗吾真言》"演技高明，言语得体"还体现在说话到位，能说到点子上。同时，讲究说话的分寸和注意自己的身份，也就是知道什么话是自己该讲的，什么话是自己不该讲的，应该讲到什么程度。

\<Zongwu's word\>In courtesy talking, the first step is greeting. Good greeting is good for your talking and make counterpart feel warm. Otherwise, the counterpart will fell not happy or angry to make both parties embarrassment.

\<Zongwu's word\>How to apply the above rule? You must get to the point whilst pay attention to your social status. In short, you must understand what can say, what can't say and to what extent.

Rule 5:
Obey to one's opinion to make stubborn donkey to chnage mind
顺毛扶驴，犟驴上套

《宗吾真言》用激将之法，让别人心甘情愿的为你办事。以激然自尊火花为目标的游说艺术，往往能在最短的时间内激发巨大的动力。

《宗吾真言》如果你的想法从根本上讲与对方的心意背道而驰，而对方又是一个犟驴，这时你绝不能说出真实的目的，犟驴发起脾气来，吃不了是要兜着走。你必须隐藏真实目的，让对方不知不觉为你出力。

<Zongwu's word>You can goad someone into action to work with you. You can motivate one in short period immensely by igniting self-esteem.

<Zongwu's word>If your idea runs in the opposite direction with one, and he is a stubborn donkey, then you can not tell about your real purpose. You must hide your real intention and let him work for you unconsciously.

Rule 6:
Satify one's vanity & give one sufficient face
满足虚荣，留足面子

《宗吾真言》"那壶不开提那壶"的说话方式是愚蠢的，揭人"伤疤"是危险的。常言道：不看憎面看佛面，尽量不能把事情做绝了。更何况多个朋友多条路，少个冤家少堵墙。

《宗吾真言》满足虚荣，留足面子还有一个方面，就是利用对方好"面子"的心理，让对方感到由于抹不开面子，不得不被牵着鼻子走，这样可以巧妙地使对方接受自己的意见。

\<Zongwu's word\>It is stupid and dangerous to expose one's scandal, dirty behavior, or shortcoming. Do not leave any room for maneuver because more friends more help more enemy more trouble.

\<Zongwu's word\>When applying the above rule, there is another factor to be considered: use one's psychology of maintaining face to lead him by the nose to accept your opinion handily.

Rule 7: Find the right solution to the case to cause sympthized

对症下药，激起共鸣

《宗吾真言》"投其所好媚人心"应针对对方的特点。在对方诸多特点中，其性格特点是最重要的考虑因素。因为，"性格决定人生"，其性格特点是和其身份、地位、行为方法直接相关的。

《宗吾真言》凡是有兴趣爱好的人，当你谈起有关他的爱好这方面的事，对方都会兴致安然。同时，对你无形中也会产生好感。因此，如果你能从中入手，发现对方特殊爱好，就会为对症下药打下良好基础。

\<Zongwu's word\>When applying code 1, you must pay attention to one's personal traits. The most important is personality because 'personality decides one's life' and relates to social status and behavior.

<Zongwu's word>If you talk about one's hobby, he will feel interest and show favor
to you. Therefore, if you can find one's hobby, it is not difficult to 'suit the remedy to the case'.

Rule 8:
Humble yourself
屈尊降贵，自贬声誉

《宗吾真言》厚黑求人者，为了达到贬低自己以抬高所求人来获取对方的好感的目的，必要时就必须"卖傻装憨"，即使受到侮辱，脸上也绝对看不出一丝一毫的不满，甚至还要装出满心欢喜的样子。

《宗吾真言》人表现的过于精明，过于完美，常常会带来麻烦，特别是身为属下，尤其如此。聪明人运用"投其所好媚人心"有时要装作糊涂，并表现出有人格的缺陷，这样才能保住自己，达到目的。

<Zongwu's word> To downgrade himself and humble himself if necessary therefore 'Thick black' person can win opponent's favor. Even he is humiliated he does not care and seems happy.

<Zongwu's word>As a subordinate if he shows excessive sharp and perfect he will get trouble. When applying code 1, clever people sometime will act dumb even shows his personal defect to protect himself and to reach his goal.

Rule 9:
Flatter to the point
溜须找须，拍到点上

《宗吾真言》世人都喜欢被人恭维，但是拍马要拍到点子上。根据"投其所好媚人心"的要求，必须按照不同人的特点，用不同的方式，讲不同的恭维话。

《宗吾真言》"溜须找须，拍到点上"有时很难，可是有时也很容易，甚至是现成摆在眼前的，比如，当人遇到不幸时，最需要别人的安慰，如果你能得体地安慰她，就等于"雪中送炭"，对方自然会非常感激你。

\<Zongwu's word\>According to the requirement of code 1, if you want to flatter someone, you should get to the point based on different personal trait, occasion and talk.

\<Zongwu's word\>Sometime it is difficult to apply above rule, however sometime it is easy based on circumstances. For instance, when misfortune happens to someone, what he needs is comfort and console. If you can comfort him adequacy he will appreciate you.

Code 2:
True or false? Is a game?
假作真时真亦假

Rule 10:
Make your logic flawless to mix the false with genuine
环环相扣，以假乱真

《宗吾真言》谎言中任何一个细节的疏漏，都可能成为他人识破谎言的关键。因此，在说谎之前，哪怕是一个最微不足道的细节也不要放过，都要设计周密，尽可能的做到滴水不漏。

《宗吾真言》人们在接到一个信息时，一般不会马上相信，他们往往通过多方渠道，以及前后发生的事情，联系起来加以印证。"谎言"想被别人信以为真，一个重要的因素，就是使用证据具有内在的逻辑性，避免前后矛盾。

<Zongwu's word>If you miss any one of details of lie it is possible to be used as a key factor to be seen through. Therefore before lie you must plan carefully even do not miss any small detail to make lie flawless.

<Zongwu's word>When someone gets information, he will not believe immediately and will verify through different channels and related matters. If you want others to believe

your lie, one important factor is: the evidence must be consistent to avoid contradiction.

Rule 11:
Ask while knowing the answer to get what you want
明知鼓昧，气定神闲

《宗吾真言》"瞎话"不说则已，要说就得"挣着眼睛"说，绝对不能"眨"眼睛。谎言编造的合乎情理，才能诱使别人深深陷进谎言的迷宫而不知回访。使谎话掷地有声，任何一句都具有鲜明的客观性，都充满了厚黑智慧。

《宗吾真言》"挣着眼睛说瞎话"的最高"修为"就是"明知鼓昧"，也就是明明知道了这件事情是假的，却能故意装着不知道，甚至自己都相信是"真"，这样才能达到"说谎"的最佳效果。

<Zongwu's word>When you lie do not blink your eyes. Make up your lie to be reasonable and full of wisdom of 'thick black', and then you can lure others to jump your trap.

<Zongwu's word>The best term for lie is 'ask while knowing the answer'. That is: you know it is false but pretend do not know even believe it is true to get the desirable result.

Rule 12:
Use public media to confound right&wrong
人言畏骨，众口铄金

《宗吾真言》别人只能看你表面的东西，内心的、背后的东西是很难看透的。只有你想让别人知道的东西，你才显露给别人，你不想让别人知道的东西，你就可以把他们藏起来。这也就说要学会做秀表演，以影响并控制舆论。

《宗吾真言》对于一些大人物，想要制造有利于自己的舆论，其中一个更直接有效的方法，就是直接掌握舆论工具。当然这个舆论工具可能是你自己的，也可能是别人的，你只是利用工作之便。

<Zongwu's word>What others can see is only your external; it is not easy to see through your internal and behind. Only you want to let others know then you can expose to others; if you do not want others to know just hide it. Therefore you should learn how to show and manipulate the media.

<Zongwu's word>For famous people if they want to make public opinion favoring to them, one of effective way is control media directly. This media can be yours or others, what you can do just use it.

Rule 13:
Add inflammatory details to the true or false
虚虚实实，添油加醋

《宗吾真言》要把"虚虚实实"的谎言效果发挥出来，可以一会儿把事情顺着说，一会儿把事情反着说，以造成对方思维的混乱，而在对方开始迷惑时，浑水摸鱼，乘机达到自己的目的。

《宗吾真言》要把"谎言"说的像，一定要运用虚实相间的技巧，也就是说，如果全是假的，别人很容易识破；如果全是真的，也就不是说假话了。最佳的策略是虚实相间，以小实掩大谎。

\<Zongwu's word\>If you want to exert the result of 'alternate with true and false' of lie, sometime you can talk in order sometime on the opposition to confuse the counterpart to get the job done.

\<Zongwu's word\>If you want others to believe your lie you must apply skillfully about 'alternate with true and false'. If all is false others will see through; if all is true, it is not lie. The best strategy is alternate with true and false, i.e. use small true to cover up big false.

Rule 14:
Fabricate evidence to win the trust
无中生有，以小充大

《宗吾真言》要想获得别人真诚的合作，就必须获得别人的信任。厚黑行世者自己都不一定信任自己，可是他们却有办法是别人相信，其中之一就是在一些"小事"上博取对方的信任，然后再"大事"上造假。

《宗吾真言》在厚黑行世中，要想引起对方的重视，就得有吸引对方的地方。而且，你手中的"王牌"一定是对方没有的东西。假如你没有这种"可居"的"奇货"，这时，你就要运用"无中生有"的办法，假造一个"奇货"。

《宗吾真言》利用"以小充大"之法，"假作真时真亦假"还有一个重要的作用，就是能够"疲敌误敌"，使强大的对手迷失方向，忘却事情的关键所在，糊里糊涂中被你牵着鼻子走。

<Zongwu's word>If you want to cooperate with others sincerely you must win trust first. Sometime 'thick black' person does not believe himself but he can make others believe. One of tactics is: get trust in small thing to make false in big matter.

<Zongwu's word>In 'thick black' society, if you want to get attention by others you had better have something to be attractive; moreover your 'trump card' must be unique. If you do not have such unique 'trump card' you can fabricate one.

<Zongwu's word>One of function of the above code is 'use small to pretend big' to confuse strong enemy to get lost. It is time to lead enemy by the nose because enemy forgets the critical matter.

Rule 15:
Deny the condemn firmly
铁嘴钢牙，死不认账

《宗吾真言》谎言终究是谎言，你企图以谎言蒙蔽对方，如果对方也是一个厚黑之士，可能对方马上就能觉察到你的意图或迹象，如果你还是一成不变的骗下去，势必到头来丢人现眼。

<Zongwu's word>Lie is lie. If the counterpart is also 'thick black' person he will see through you immediately. Therefore you should change your strategy otherwise you will get embarrassment.

Rule 16: Head off a danger with your eloquence
舌转乾坤，化险为夷

《宗吾真言》常言道："伴君如伴虎"。可是，很多中国古代的厚黑大师，在可能面临杀头之祸时，沉着冷静，察言观色，诙谐幽默，以厚黑智谋之语保存了自己的生命，并得到皇帝的赏识。现代的下属们不妨学着一试。

《宗吾真言》"舌转乾坤，化险为夷"，（火候和时机要把握得好）关键在于随机应变。而且这种"变"通常都是被动的，一般人身处险境时已下得半死，早就顾不上"变"了，更谈不上把分寸拿捏的恰到好处了。

《宗吾真言》运用""舌转乾坤，化险为夷"时，有一个问题需要注意，就是怎样不使自己的聪明过分的表现出来，以免刺激到上司的自尊心，而节外生枝、适得其反。

<Zongwu's word>It is said 'human is dangerous'. However, most ancient Chinese 'thick black' persons were rational, calm, carefully watch what somebody are doing and saying and humor to save their life and get appreciation from emperor when beheaded. Modern people should learn from them.

<Zongwu's word>The key to the above rule is 'play to the score'. This change is tough because ordinary people scare to death in dangerous situation, how to talk about change even more applying skillful.

<Zongwu's word>When applying above rule you must pay attention to one issue: never flaunt your sharp to hurt your boss' esteem to get trouble.

Rule 17: Deny the question with the mere verbal statement
空口无凭, 循迹匿形

《宗吾真言》如果能做到"空口无凭"当然最好, 可是, 有时别人不但不相信自己的谎言, 还提出质疑, 拿出了证据怎么办? 有时可以采用一些文字游戏, 以示对方的证据失效。如断章取义、语意双关等文字游戏, 没准可以改变被动局面。

<Zongwu's word>If you can deny 'the mere verbal statement' it is good. However, sometime others not only do not believe your lie but also question even more come out with evidence, how? Sometime you can adopt paronomasia to invalidate the evidence, for example, 'quote out of context', 'double meaning' etc, maybe you can turn around.

Rule 18: Transfer the fraud to turn adversity
偷梁换柱, 顺势反击

《宗吾真言》"欲加之罪，何患无辞"，这是权力支配者对被支配者的一种"假作真时真亦假"的手法； 如果同等地位而要陷害对方的话，那就是"欲加之罪，何患无计"了。自己不用出面，又达到了自己的目的。

《宗吾真言》遭到重大挫折，仅凭自己的力量无法恢复，为了能够东山再起，利用一切可以利用的事物，从另外的地方，以另外的形式重新出现。 这就是"借尸还魂"，此招用于"顺势反击"在合适不过。

《宗吾真言》运用"偷梁换柱，顺势反击"的说谎技巧，必须在对方不知不觉中，用某种东西换走另一种东西。调换的时候，一般都是用假的换掉真的，用坏的换掉好的，用次要的换掉主要的。 当对方发现受骗上当时，已经来不及了。

<Zongwu's word>It is easy to find fault. That's the common approach of official dominators use above code. If you want to set up your peer you still can use above code. Just use others advantage to get what you want without wasting resources.

<Zongwu's word>When you get setback and can't recover just of your own strength, you can use others help to bob up like a cork. That's the 'revive in a new guise' to turn adversity.

<Zongwu's word>When applying above rule, you should exchange something with another from the counterpart unconsciously. Normally is: use false to change true, bad to good, minor to major. It is too late when the counterpart finds out that he is cheated.

Code 3:
Attack by innuendo to touch one
含沙射影动以情

Rule 19:
Know the real situation to ease tension
摸清底牌，消除对抗

《宗吾真言》要视对方完全改变自己的意志，必须摸清对方的思维脉络，然后顺着对方的思路来哄骗他，这样对方就会心甘情愿的改变自己的意志。

《宗吾真言》哄骗对方的一个基本前提就是使对方相信你是在为他着想，只有这样，他才会接受你的意见。反之，如果对方的心理武装没有解除，那么你的一切说辞，对方都会提出质疑。

<Zongwu's word>If you want to change ones mind you must understand his thinking, and then follow his thinking to hoax him. In this way he is willing to change his mind.

<Zongwu's word>The basic premise to hoax someone is to make him believe that you consider for him. Only this he can accept your opinion. On the other hand if he does not release his arm he will question what you say.

Rule 20:
Build good relationship
to get what you want
以情之矛，攻情之盾

《宗吾真言》在社会的每一件事，都在明里暗中交织在错综复杂的关系网中。因此，一定要善于运用关系网，有了熟人，才有人情，有了人情，才好说话，你的口才才可以淋漓发挥，你的目的才能顺利达到。

《宗吾真言》如果对方有错在先，自知理亏，这时如果你能采用一种"得饶人处且饶人"的姿态，甚至做到以德报怨，对方通常会马上改变态度和观点。因此，以德报怨是"以情之矛，攻情之盾"的一个重要方面。

《宗吾真言》如果你曾有恩于对方，或者对方曾经欠你人情，你在说服对方时，一定要善于用这一点打动他，设法使对方重新升起对你的歉疚之情，这时你的情感攻势就很容易成功。

<Zongwu's word>In this world everything is related and complicated. Therefore you must be good at using relationship network. If you have more acquaintances and friends, you have more relationship, and then you can exert your eloquence to reach your goal.

<Zongwu's word>If someone knows his mistake and admit it, at this time if you forgive him even 'return good foe evil', he will change his attitude and idea at once. Therefore 'return good for evil' is one of important factor of above rule.

<Zongwu's word>If you are the benefactor to someone or he owed you something, when you want to persuade him you had better use it to let him feel guilty. Finally you will succeed.

Rule 21:
Beat about the bush
to win his heart
旁敲侧击，触动心灵

《宗吾真言》要把一个现成的结论强加给对方很难，但却可以很容易地把推理和思维的程序"推销"给对方，这时，只要点拨一下问题的症结所在，对方就很自然的沿着你指定的思路得出结论。

《宗吾真言》有权有势的人一般都非常自负，不大愿意接受别人的意见，这时要触动他们心灵就得用更巧妙的办法。不妨试一试类比和比喻的方法，是对方悟出假如不按你所说的去做，后果非常严重。

《宗吾真言》要说服愚顽不化的人，最好是让他自己得出结论。如果能让他自己惊出一身冷汗，效果更佳。这时可以顺着对方的逻辑，把对方行为后果夸张放大，直至荒缪的程度，使对方自省。

<Zongwu's word>It is difficult to force your opinion to others. But it is easy to promote your reasoning and thinking. At the meantime if you remind the key problem he will follow your thinking to get conclusion.

<Zongwu's word>People with high power are conceited normally and do not accept others idea. Therefore you must use smart way to touch their heart. Try analogy and metaphor to make them realize that if they do not follow your advice they will bear serious consequences.

<Zongwu's word>If you want to persuade stubborn one the best way is let him conclude himself. If you can let him scare to cold sweat the result is better. Then you can follow his

logic to exaggerate the consequence even to ridicule to let him reflect.

Rule 22:
Use benefit to lure his desire
利益刺激，勾起欲望

《宗吾真言》运用"利益刺激，勾起欲望"这一手法，把对方的胃口吊起来，激发起他的兴趣，并不一定意味着其已改变自己的意志或意见，这时必须不断的激发，以巩固"兴奋点"，促成其改变想法。

<Zongwu's word>When applying the above rule you must give suspense and inspire ones interest. However, it does not mean that he has changed his will or idea. Therefore you must inspire constantly to reinforce 'excitement point' to change his idea.

Rule 23:
Pretend helpless to win his compassion
装扮弱者，换取同情

《宗吾真言》人类天生就会同情弱者，这时人类的弱点。调动眼泪战法，对人哀哀以求，动之以情，这种求人术，古今中外都有。

《宗吾真言》常言道，"男儿有泪不轻弹"。 男子汉大丈夫哭鼻子实在不雅，有失风度，但男人若肯放下面子，大流眼泪，效果更强。只是男子汉若哭必须厚脸皮。

《宗吾真言》"装扮弱者，换取同情"也要讲究策略。

<Zongwu's word>Human sympathize incompetent person by nature. That's the weakness of human. Therefore you should use your tears and sorrow to plea to win compassion.

<Zongwu's word>It is said "man can't cry'. It is true. It is disgrace if man cry. But if man can put down his face to cry the result is better. The only way is: man must have 'thick-skinned' to cry.

<Zongwu's word>You must have your strategy when applying above rule.

Rule 24:
Strike while iron is hot in critical stage
紧要关头，趁热打铁

《宗吾真言》要想抓住机会，促成对方思想转变，必须能够发现对方心理的微妙变化，否则到了嘴边的肉又溜走了。这就必须注意观察对方，通过观察获取的大量信息，迅速反馈到大脑，迅速想出"紧要关头，趁热打铁"的措施。

《宗吾真言》在经过艰巨的说服工作，对方发出了打算接受你的意见的信息，这时，很多人会误以为大局已定，于是在精神方面放松了，语言也变得随便起来。这是很危险的，这时更需要"紧要关头，趁热打铁。"

《宗吾真言》使对方最终完全接受你的意见，要使他相信你的想法不仅在感情是合理的，而且在理智上也是正确的。因此，还必须运用语言技巧，打消对方的重要顾虑，使其最后下定决心，完成思想意志的转变。

<Zongwu's word>If you want to seize opportunity to change ones mind you must good at identifying ones subtle psychological change. Otherwise the opportunity will slide away. Therefore you should observe carefully to obtain

abundant information, then feedback to your head quickly and find out the solution.

<Zongwu's word>Through arduous persuading the counterpart sends out signal to accept your idea. At the moment most people misunderstand that everything is ok and relax. It is dangerous. You must apply the rule even more.

<Zongwu's word>If you want one to accept your idea completely you must make him believe that your idea is not only reasonable in sensation but also correct in rationality. Therefore you must apply talk technique to eliminate his worry, and finally let him make determination to change his opinion.

Rule 25: Show a firm character behind a gentle appearance to attack one's core weakness
绵里藏针，轻刺要害

《宗吾真言》厚黑行世者最惯用的手法就是示弱求怜。但是，如果能在示弱的过程中，若隐若现的流露出一点自己的实力，以增加对方的猜疑，使对方摸不着头脑，在患得患失中"不战而屈人之兵"，实现了你的意愿，则是上上之策。

《宗吾真言》对付敌人，当然希望泰山压顶，一举全歼。但是如果敌人十分强大呢？尤其是在说服别人的过程中，所要对付的不是敌人，而是朋友、友军或者需要长期维持又好关系的客户，这时不妨来个绵力相迎，以柔克刚。

<Zongwu's word>The most common approach for 'thick black' person is show weakness to get compassion. However, when showing weakness if you expose some strength to confuse someone to get your will. That's the best strategy.

\<Zongwu's word>You want to eliminate enemy thoroughly. However, if enemy is very strong, how? Especially when persuading others what you deal is not enemy but friend or long-term relationship customers, this time you can apply above rule.

Rule 26 :
Make a detour to change his mind
迂回委婉, 步步深入

《宗吾真言》人们常说，"某某说话能噎死人"说明说话太直接容易使人一时难以接受。 使用"迂回委婉，步步深入"之法就不同了， 委婉一点， 含蓄一点， 使对方悟到那层意思， 给双方考虑空间， 反而容易让人接受。

《宗吾真言》"迂回委婉， 步步深入"的说话技巧， 实质上也就是兵法上的"以迂为直,以患为利"， 舍近求远， 看似走了弯路， 实则为可行的捷径; 先于后取， 看似把"好处"给了别人， 实则自己受益。

《宗吾真言》运用"迂回委婉， 步步深入"的过程中， 可以先把自己的目的隐藏起来， 而在于对方的对话中让对方跟着自己的意思走， 最终在浑然不觉中同意了自己的意见， 而且不露声色， 了无痕迹。

\<Zongwu's word>Sometime it is not easy to accept direct and honest talk. But if you use above rule, that is different. Therefore talk in circumbendibus and connotation to let one know the point, give both parties time to consider; finally it is easy to accept.

\<Zongwu's word>The technique of above rule, in substance is the same as war-of-art. It seems detour but actually is shortcut; give first then receive. It seems give benefit to others but finally you.

<Zongwu's word>When applying above rule you should hide your real purpose and let someone follow your idea in talk, finally let him agree your idea unconsciously.

Rule 27: Use soft and hard tactics to convince him by reasoning
软中带硬，以理服人

《宗吾真言》如果你的意见或建议直接关系到对方的锦绣前程或身家性命，而你的道理又无可辩驳，对方是不会过分在乎你的态度的，换言之，对方容忍程度是因为观点的重要性和正确性而发生变化。

《宗吾真言》以理服人，并不一定代表"理直气壮"。 人人都想把自己的观点推销给对方，于是往往便很直接很肯定的告诉对方应该如何说，好像自己就是真理的化身。这样的结果往往不好。若你能找出台阶给对方体面的下，这样，你就从心理上已经说服了对方，接受你的意见就是个时间的问题了。

<Zongwu's word>If your opinion or advice concerns to ones future or life and your reasoning is unbeatable, he does not care about your attitude. In other word, his tolerance will change according to the importance and correctness of your opinion.

<Zongwu's word>Convincing people by reasoning does not mean 'one is assured and bold with justice'. Everyone wants to promote idea to others and tell others how and what to say. Actually the result is not desirable. If you can find step down for others, actually you convince others in psychology, accepting your idea just needs time.

Code 4:
False affection, real friendship to move one
虚情实意动真心

Rule 28:
Internerate opponent
to gain compassion
软化对手，博取同情

《宗吾真言》一个情场老手，为了表达对一个女人的爱，除了在枕边床上耳热身软之外，隔三差五，还得买点小花之类。即使她感到你靠不住，也会感动地再流一回泪。

《宗吾真言》要发挥"软化对手，博取同情"的作用，善套近乎是非常重要的。如果一个人具备与人一见如故的功夫，对方即使队他的话题再不感兴趣，似乎也不忍掉走开，有了这样一个好的结局，后面的话就好说了。

《宗吾真言》为了达到"软化对手，博取同情"的目的，还有一种极为有效的手段，就是通过自己的忍让，使对方感到过意不去，激起对方的同情心，自然也就原谅你了。

<Zongwu's word>To show love to his woman a love expert often buy flower for her besides sex. Even she feel that he is not the people to be counted on she will still move to tears.

<Zongwu's word>If you want to exert the function of above rule you should be skill at getting close relationship. If you have skill to meet people 'like old friends at the first meeting' one cannot bear to leave even he is not interested in your

topic. Having such good talking environment it is not difficult to talk further.

\<Zongwu's word\>Another effective way to get the purpose of above rule is self-surrender to let someone feel guilty and compassion to forgive you naturally.

Rule 29: Just act only
逢场作戏，不动真情

《宗吾真言》如果给予对方" 母亲般的温情"，正可以弥补对方游子的思乡情怀。

《宗吾真言》"逢场作戏，不动真情"还有一个特殊用法，也是最原始的用法，就是"美人计"。有人把"酒、色、财、气"喻为人生四大关口，这四大关口中" 色"关是最难过的。

\<Zongwu's word\>If you can give someone 'mother's warmth' it can remedy his homesick.

\<Zongwu's word\>The special usage or the most original usage is 'beauty trick'. Someone allegorizes 'alcohol, beauty, money and spirit' as life four passes. The most difficult pass is beauty.

Rule 30: Blame adequatly to convinc
批驳有度，无话可说

《宗吾真言》有的人在批评时，总是夸大其词，借机整人，往往以一时一事的失误，就将人的过去全盘否定，觉得此人

"朽木不可雕也"，甚至当面断定对方"不可救药"。这么想和这么说都是大错特错。

《宗吾真言》批评别人时，如果时机不对，会带来一系列消极的影响。一定要善于把握批评的时机。对于这种时机把握，一定要以对方容易接受你的意见为前提。

《宗吾真言》在进行有效批评时，除了考虑原则、方式和时机之外，还必须注意对批评的艺术性的考量，使自己在反驳对方不适当的言行时有的放矢，效果明显。

\<Zongwu's word\>When someone criticizes others, he always likes to exaggerate to set up others. Normally he picks on small mistake to deny all others accomplishments even conclude others are 'beyond redemption'. What he thinks and what he says is blunder.

\<Zongwu's word\>If you can't pick the suitable time to criticize others it will caused serious negative effect. Therefore you should grasp the right time to criticize. The premise is someone is willing to accept your idea.

\<Zongwu's word\>When you criticize you must consider principle, manner, opportunity and state-of-art to get desirable result.

Rule 31:
Open mind, forestall your opponent by a show of strength
开诚布公，先声夺人

《宗吾真言》在说服对方的过程中，不要回避利益这个核心问题，采用开城布公的方法，客观地分析对方行动的利与弊，设法使对方的某种需要得以满足，从而使自己的需要也得到满足。

《宗吾真言》"开诚布公"打着为对方着想的旗号的确不失为一个好办法。但是，你得有机会在对方面前陈述其中厉害。因此，必须以出人意料的手段，引起对方注意。

《宗吾真言》如果对方不肯轻易顺服你的意见，甚至显出一种居高临下的姿态时，你可以示弱乞连，然后步入正题；也可以开始一上来就以"先声夺人"之势压制对方，从而让对方屈从和改变主意，这就是反客为主。

<Zongwu's word>When persuading someone you do not avoid the key issue of benefit. You can open mind and analyze cost/benefit of his action, try your best to satisfy his partial need and finally satisfy your need.

<Zongwu's word>'Open mind' means consider for someone, however you must crab the chance to demonstrate the fearfulness to him. Therefore you must bear all means to cause his attention.

<Zongwu's word>If someone does not want to follow your idea even show his commanding. You can show your weakness and plea, then go to the subject; you can also 'forestall your opponent by a show of strength' to suppress opponent, thus ask opponent to give in and change his idea.

Rule 32: Say 'no' is an art
敢于拒绝，善于说不

《宗吾真言》很多人不认识"不"字的伟大，遇事优柔寡断，畏首畏尾，结果使自己处于被动地位，听命于人。说出这个"不"真的这么困难吗？其实，要说"不"，并非直言起"不"，还可以语中藏"不"。

<Zongwu's word>Most people do not know the greatness of "No". When something happens to him he shows indecision and flinch to make him difficulty to obey others. Is it real difficult to say "No"? Actually, you do not say it directly and say it in hidden.

Rule 33:
To be generous to win one's heart
不吝赏赐，收买人心

《宗吾真言》为了使下属保持忠诚，上司必须常常想着下属，尊敬他，使他富贵，使他感恩戴德，让他分享荣誉，承担职责。同时，也使他知道如果没有自己，他就站不住，这样他就会心甘情愿地为你买命。

《宗吾真言》人活在世上有的时候为了名可以舍利，可以忘生。因此，在运用"不吝赏赐，收买人心"这一"虚情实意动真心"的技巧时，别忘了"世人重名"这一本性。

<Zongwu's word>To keep subordinate loyalty boss must consider him, respect him, make him wealthy, and let him share success and bear responsibility and make him feel deeply grateful. At the meantime let him know that he can't get foothold without you. In this way he will be most willing to work for you.

<Zongwu's word>Sometime people can give up gain and life for fame. Therefore when apply above rule do not forget that most people pay attention to fame.

Rule 34:
Apologize sincerely to gain forgiveness
诚心道歉，求得谅解

《宗吾真言》是人就难免犯错误，能否求得谅解关键看你的态度。如果采取拒不认帐的态度，能推就推，能躲就躲，以为可以不为后果负责，保住了面子，又避免了损失。实际上往往适得其返。

以坦率地承认过失来显示诚心是最佳策略。拒不认账的结果是弊大于利。首先，铸成的大错是近人皆知的，抵赖只能让人觉得你没有骨气。

《宗吾真言》当由于自己的过错而给别人造成了损失时，应当致以诚心的歉意。那么如何表现自己的诚心呢？你不妨也过分拔高自己的错误，使对方感到不好意思追究你的责任。这是"虚情实意动真心"的一个妙招。

《宗吾真言》有人能够充分认识到道歉的重要性，也认识到自己的错误，也诚心想要道歉，就是躲躲闪闪，羞羞答答不知如何开口。这就要用巧妙的说话艺术了。

<Zongwu's word>Human can make mistake. Forgive or not depends on your attitude. If you think by denying mistake to avoid responsibility, keep face and avoid loss, it is wrong. The best strategy is candid to admit fault to show sincerely. The result of denying mistake is cost higher than benefit. Because everyone knows your mistake, denying means you do not have moral integrity.

<Zongwu's word>When your fault causes other's loss, you should apologize sincerely. How to show you're sincerely? You may overstate your fault to make someone feel guilty to blame your responsibility. This is the clever technique of above code.

<Zongwu's word>Someone knows the importance of apology, recognize his mistake and want to apologize sincerely, but he is shy and does not know how to say. Therefore he should use art-of-talk.

Rule 35 : Solve complaint to aviod misunderstanding 消除抱怨，避免误解

《宗吾真言》求得别人的谅解从本质上说就是解除自己的困境。但是大错已成，如何扭转局面？办法就是"虚情实意动真心"。可是这里有个前提，就是有效沟通。如果不能有效沟通，其他的无从谈起了。

《宗吾真言》在进行有效的沟通之后，就要有针对性地用""虚情实意动真心"来求得对方的谅解。如果这种局面是由于误解造成的，就要尽量解释清楚，消除误解。

《宗吾真言》如果你的行为造成了对方的不满，引起了对方的抱怨，要想求得谅解，就必须化解这种抱怨，特别是对于必须维持长期良好关系的双方来说，化解抱怨就意味着事业的发展。

<Zongwu's word>In substance asking forgiveness means eliminate your difficulty. But if you made a big mistake how to turn around? The solution is above code. The premise is effective communication. If you can't communicate effectively it is not necessary to talk about others.

<Zongwu's word>After effective communication you should apply above code pertinently to ask forgiveness of opponent. If this situation is incurred by misunderstanding you should explain clearly to eliminate misunderstanding.

<Zongwu's word>If your behavior causes opponent's unhappy and complaint, you want to get forgiveness you

must solve the complaint. Especially for long-term good relationship customers solving complaint means your business expansion.

Rule 36 : Go in hot persuit to conquer your opponent 穷追猛打，降伏对手

《宗吾真言》如何回答握有生杀大权的上司的话，本身就不是一件容易的事。如果这时又有同僚告黑状，你的处境就非常险恶了。当面对这种情况时，运用"穷追猛打"同样可以降伏对手，转危为安，变祸为福。

<Zongwu's word>It is not easy to answer your boss who controls your destiny suitably. At the meantime if your peer complaint you, your situation is dangerous. Well, you can apply above rule to turn adversity.

Rule 37 :
Still water runs deep,
Show your good and hiden you evil
大智若愚，藏恶露善

《宗吾真言》运用" 藏恶露善，大智若愚" 时，可以装傻为人遮羞，自找台阶， 可以故做不知，反唇相讥；可以装痴不癫，迷惑对手。但必须演的真实，傻的可爱，"疯"的恰到好处。

《宗吾真言》如果说话的对象是一个不讲道理而又大权在握的人，这时"藏恶露善，大智若愚" 特别有效，既可达到说话的目的， 又可不触动"龙麟"而引祸伤身。

《宗吾真言》在辩论时，面对对手的围攻，对别人的话装作没有听到或没有听清楚，以便实施避实就虚。 这种说辩兴致使之无法继续设置被动局面。

<Zongwu's word>When applying above rule you can pretend silly to cover up your embarrassment, find the step down, pretend do not know and talk back. But you must act like celebrity, be stupid but adorable, and be crazy but just right.

<Zongwu's word>if your opponent is unreasonable with super power it is special effective to apply above rule. In this way you get what you say but never touch him to get trouble.
<Zongwu's word>In debate when you opponent attack you, you pretend can't hear or can't hear clearly to implement 'alternate with true and false'. This can set up difficulty situation to discontinue the debate.

Rule 38:
Deliberate to expose
your rip and ugly
故露破绽，出丑卖乖

《宗吾真言》这里的" 鼓露破绽，出丑卖乖"是主动为之，主动权就掌握在自己手中，换句话说，这里的"破绽"和"丑"是有选择的，是故意让对方看见，以便转移其对真正的"破绽"和"丑"的注意力。

《宗吾真言》" 鼓露破绽"之术，还有另一种运用方法：有意识地通过看似失语的语言形式，"无意"的透露给听话者某种虚假的信息，从而使对方信以为真，以正中说话者的下怀。

<Zongwu's word>When applying above rule you select rip and ugly and show to opponent to transfer his attention to real rip and ugly.

<Zongwu's word>Another application for above rule: deliberate expose false information to opponent through a slip of the tongue to make opponent to believe it is true to hit your desire.

Rule 39:
Hide your smart, show your clumsy
自愚扮笨, 藏巧示拙

《宗吾真言》官场上经常两派形同水火、势不两立，冤家对头，他们之所以斗的个你死我活，归根结底，还是为了权、利两字。但对于厚黑行世者，真正的对手不是"政敌"，而是居于他们之上的人。所以，千万不要"功高震主"。

《宗吾真言》当一个人权是正隆时，千万不要以为那是永远不会衰败的。要清醒地认识到，在那烈火煎油般的鼎盛中，已预伏了危机，已埋下了祸根。厚黑行世者，必须预作安排，该放弃的就放弃，以避免祸难。

<Zongwu's word>Two parties often fight and scheme each other for fame and gain in officialdom. But for 'thick black' person the real enemy is not his rival but his boss. Therefore never outperform your boss.

<Zongwu's word>When someone's power is on hill do not assume that he will not be over the hill. Therefore he must recognize there are crisis and disaster over there in this complex competitive environment. For 'thick black' person he must predict that and give up if necessary.

Rule 40:
Just get to the point
点到为止, 出语必中

《宗吾真言》厚黑行世者，在设计"陷阱"打击对手时，一定要考虑到其中的风险。在揣摩好上司的意图后，不直接表达心愿，而是利用"点到为止，出语必中"之法，置购陷于赞扬之中，使其有苦难言，而自己又保留了一条抽身之路。

<Zongwu's word>The 'thick black' person must consider the risk when he tries to set up opponent. After analyze boss' intention he uses above rule to talk hidden and praise his boss to make his boss hard to save his life.

Rule 41:
To be thick-skinned
to be derided and taunted
笑骂由人，厚脸不红

《宗吾真言》只有真正聪明的人才能驾驶语言艺术，而自嘲又是语言艺术的最高境界。在人前蒙羞，处境尴尬时，用自嘲来对付，就能很容易找到台阶。所以，能够自嘲并能自我解嘲是一种很高明的"防人脱身"手段。

《宗吾真言》当你的失误引发对立情绪时，如果能适时地自嘲一番，获得原谅应该不难。这就像两个打架的人，一个突然故意倒地自认不是对手，如果对方不是无赖恶棍，一般便会又好气又好笑的敌意顿消。

<Zongwu's word>Only real sharp people can manipulate talk-of-art, mock oneself is the best of the art. When he shows disgrace and embarrassment he can use mock to handle and find the step down easily. Therefore mock one and try to explain things away when been mocked is the good way to protect oneself.

<Zongwu's word>When your mistake causes tension if you can mock yourself it is not difficult to get forgiveness. Just like two persons fight each other, if one falls down suddenly and admit defected the other one will forgive if he is not a rascal.

135

Rule 42:
Be gentle to everyone to have the Initiate
八面玲珑，掌握主动

《宗吾真言》在争夺权力非常复杂的环境中，你一定有同党，也有敌人和大量的中间派。如果善于"八面玲珑，掌握主动"，利用在某个问题上的共同利益，分化瓦解后两类人，为己所用，去收拾异己。

<Zongwu's word>In this complicated environment when you fight for power you should have compliance, enemy and vast middle-party. If you can use above rule, disintegrate the latter two people for common interest. It is not difficult to get rid of your enemy.

Rule 43:
Look one way and row another
隐真示假，声东击西

《宗吾真言》有时光蒙是蒙不住的。这时不妨用"虚拟示意"的论辩技巧，将本来没有的情况当做客观事实推出，并竭力让对手相信。这样，同样可以让对方真假难辨。

《宗吾真言》运用"隐真示假，声东击西"之法，还可以通过虚张声势，故意假装强大的声势来吓唬人。

<Zongwu's word>Sometime you can't always cheat others. Therefore you should apply above rule to treat false as true to make opponent believe. Thus you can confuse the opponent.

<Zongwu's word>When applying above rule, you can pretend strong to scare enemy through bravado.

Rule 44:
Change consantly to suit the environment
敌变我变，顺势而变

《宗吾真言》"识时务者为俊杰"，天地日月，自然万物，无时无刻不在变化。生存在变化的环境中，我们也在不知不觉的变化着。因此，在运用"防人之心不可无"时，一定要"相对而动，欲擒故纵"。

《宗吾真言》处理任何事情都要学会掌握节奏的变化。要达到某一目的，不能直冲着目标而去，碰了南墙也不回头，而应学会迂回环绕。面对一座极为陡峭的高山险峰，不要冒险去直接援壁而上，可以绕定。着山路环行，最后便可安全的到达山顶。

<Zongwu's word>Change is ongoing all the time. When applying above code you must change to 'leave somebody at large the better to apprehend him'.

<Zongwu's word>If you want to handle something you must master rhythmical change. Want to reach your goal you must learn how to detour to get the peak of mountain safety.

Rule 45:
Alert and keep a lookout always
时时自警，防患未然

《宗吾真言》世人都有一种虚荣心里，一旦位居高官享富贵之极，便极尽表现之能事，处处显耀，让人觉得不可一世，大有天下惟我独尊之势。殊不知树大招风，这样的炫耀极有可能为自己招来灾祸，甚至是灭顶之灾。

<Zongwu's word>Human has vanity in nature. When someone is in high power to enjoy his riches and honor he always flaunts himself and shows extremely conceited. However, he will get trouble even disaster.

Code 6:
Use your word to distress one without physical injury
语箭伤人不见血

Rule 46:
Treat sb. with the way one has devised against others; Success will come when conditions ripe
请君入瓮, 水到渠成

《宗吾真言》强弩百步之内可以穿金削铁，而到千步之外时，就会绵纸不破，这是因为超过了力量的极限。"因其强而强之乃可折页，因其广而广之乃可缺也。"运用"语箭"时，同样要善于造成于已有利，与敌有害的态势。

《宗吾真言》在中国古代的诡辩术中，有这样一种方法，为了反对某一观点，首先表示热烈赞同，然后对其大加发挥，引向极端，使人一听就知道其中谬误百出，从而达到不攻自破的目的。

《宗吾真言》军事谋略中有一条妙计，叫"将欲弱之，必姑强之；将欲取之，必姑予之。"其中的"强"和"予"，就是纵敌失去节制，造成"物及必反"的后果。这一招对于处于劣势、困境中的说话一方面，同样非常实用。

<Zongwu's word>The crossbow can cut iron and metal within one hundred steps however it can do nothing beyond thousand steps because of out of limit. Therefore when you

139

apply above rule you must be good at creating situation favoring to you unfavorable to enemy.

<Zongwu's word>In ancient Chinese special pleading there is one way: to oppose the opponent's opinion you agree at the beginning then exaggerate to the extreme. After that the opponent will identify the falsehood obviously to change his mind.

<Zongwu's word>There is a wonderful technique in military strategy: 'Strengthen first then weaken; give first then take'. Here 'strengthen' and 'give' means to make enemy lose control to go to 'extremes meet'. It is useful for weakness and difficulty side.

Rule 47:
Use one's friend to remove one's barrier without wasting resources
引友杀敌，不出自力

《宗吾真言》运用"引友杀敌，不出自力"这一招，自己既可以不被发现，又可以在危急的时候，嫁祸于人。为了保存自己的实力，而利用矛盾，必须巧妙的借用第三方的力量。而最高明的"借"， 就借敌人的力量打击敌人。

《宗吾真言》运用"引友杀敌"之计，一个关键在于能否把第三方力量"借"来。否则，就像孙悟空借芭蕉扇一样，借得一把假扇，用来灭火不成，反倒烧了自己。诱借就是一种有效方法，利用各种引诱之法，使其自愿上钩，情愿主动地被借用。

<Zongwu's word>When applying above rule, you can hide and transfer the misfortune in emergence. To save energy and use conflict you must be good at borrowing the third party's

power. The best one is to borrow enemy's power to defect another enemy.

<Zongwu's word>When applying above rule, the key is whether you can borrow third party's power or not. Otherwise you will burn yourself like Sun wukong. Luring to borrow is an effective way to make opponent borrow to you on his own will.

Rule 48: Make use of every bit of time or space to intensify conflict 见缝插针，激化矛盾

《宗吾真言》运用"见缝插针，激化矛盾"时，可以想方设法破坏异己与那些同异己比较亲密的人之间的关系，使他们的关系由亲密转向生疏，由信任变为猜疑，扩大两者之间的矛盾，增加两者之间的不信任。

《宗吾真言》如果对手之间互相勾结，就会形成较强大的势力。只要对手铁板一块，自己就无机可乘。如果采取制造矛盾，分而至之等手段诱使其自相牵制，不但削弱其实力，还可以为自己创造可乘之机。

<Zongwu's word>When applying above rule, you cast about to breach close relationship with opponent and make their relationship from close to strange, from trust to doubt, and finally they suspect each other.

<Zongwu's word>If opponent cahoots they will unite to strength. Therefore you do not have any chance to attack. If you fabricate conflict to lure them hold down each other you can weaken their strength to make the chance to attack.

Rule 49:
Show loyalty and consideration to one's boss to get what you want
小遵大违，小信大诡

《宗吾真言》在生活上对上司体贴入微，这样上司就会相信你的忠诚。如此一来，在大事上对上司进行蒙蔽就容易了。这时，在想办法实施与己有利、与上司不利的事。

《宗吾真言》运用"小遵大违，小信大诡"之法，要善于揣摩上司的意图，不管上司的决策如何错误，只要于你有利，便积极支持，马上落实，看似对上司忠心耿耿，实质上最后把上司推向灭亡。

<Zongwu's word>If you care about your boss life details he will believe your loyalty. Then you can cheat him in big issue. After that you implement plan favoring to you unfavorable to him.

<Zongwu's word>When applying above rule, you must skill in analyzing your boss intention. No matter any mistake of his decision if it is favor to you, you must support and implement immediately. It looks you are loyal to him but actually you drive him to the dead end.

Rule 50:
Stop communication to one's boss to the real situation
闭目塞听，阻断沟通

《宗吾真言》一人之下，万人之上的"权臣"，所畏惧的只有上司。但如果上司不知道他做了什么事，就谁也不怕。所以，只要让上司闭目塞听、杜绝言路，外事不知，就可以只手遮天了。

《宗吾真言》如果能把"小遵大违，小信大诡"与"闭目塞听，阻断沟通"结合起来，"语箭伤人不见血"的威力就更大了。

<Zongwu's word>Above thousands people but below only one is 'powerful and imperious officials', what he fears is his boss. But if his boss does not know what he has done therefore he is fearless. Therefore if he stops communication to his boss he can do everything.

<Zongwu's word>If you can apply rule 49 and rule 50, there is more power of code 6.

Rule 51:
Fabricate excuse and set up trap
制造口实，张网设局

《宗吾真言》"制造口实，张网设局"要事先经过周密的安排，激化，给对方挖好陷阱、设好圈套。再想办法将对手引入陷阱之内、圈套之中，这样一来，异己就像凶猛的老虎失去锋利的牙齿一样，只能任人宰割。

《宗吾真言》"制造口实，张网设局"从某种意义上说，是一种"借刀杀人"的计谋。通过"馋诬"借助上司的力量搬倒对手。一般来说，本人是不会直接出面与对手进行面对面的正面交锋，而且往往还作出推心置腹、亲密无间的姿态，使对手放松警惕。

<Zongwu's word>When applying above rule, you must plan in details and set up trap for opponent, then lure the opponent to your trap. In this way your opponent will like 'ferocious tiger' that lost his sharp teeth to be manipulated.

<Zongwu's word>From some points the above rule is a strategy of 'use others to remove your barrier'. You can borrow boss power to remove your opponent through badmouth. In general, you need not fight with your opponent face-to-face even show your confidant to your opponent to loosen his alert.

Rule 52:
Use eisegesis to trap one's rival
牵强附会，名敌为贼

《宗吾真言》运用"语箭伤人不见血"之法打击对手时，是不会直来直去的，如果是这样，对手会有所防备。使用"牵强附会，名敌为贼"之计就不同了，这样可以使对手在迷迷糊糊中着了你的道。

《宗吾真言》如果你与竞争对手是同一级别的同事，同样可以采用"牵强附会，名敌为贼"之法，使你的上司逐渐对你的竞争对手产生厌恶的感觉，最终在你们的竞争中，站在你这一方。

《宗吾真言》使用"牵强附会，名敌为贼"之法，使别人站到你的一边，这种方法固然有效，但是，常言道"纸里包不住火"，一旦对手有了解释的机会，你的这一招术就不功子破了。

<Zongwu's word>When applying above code to attack your opponent, you need not be face-to-face; otherwise the opponent will defend himself. However it is difference to apply above rule you can confuse opponent.

<Zongwu's word>If your rival is your peer you still can apply above rule to make your boss dislike your rival. Finally your boss will stand in your side in your competition.

<Zongwu's word>When applying above rule to make others support you, it works. However, if rival gets the chance to explain it does not work.

Rule 53: Make false report against rival to confuse one's boss
鼓弄唇舌，搅混池水

《宗吾真言》在上司面前说自己对手的坏话，汇报对同僚不利的情况，叫打" 小报告"。通常情况下，这些"小报告"都是虚假的，不真实的；凡是真实的或有事实根据的都不称为"小报告"。

总之，预先探听到对手的一些情况，然后采取打'小报告"方式，使上司曲解对手的下步行动，不仅可以打击对手，还可以在上司的心中增加自己的分量。

《宗吾真言》"鼓弄唇舌，搅混池水" 这一手法的表现形式是多种多样的：有无中生有、故意捏造的；有信口开河、缺乏事实根据的；有以假充真、以偏盖全，以一真掩九假的。但是，无论以什么形式，其内容从实质上都是虚假的。

<Zongwu's word>To badmouth your rival and make a false report to your peer calls 'lodge a complaint against someone to his boss'. Normally it is false. Therefore you should investigate your rival some materials then make false report to cause your boss distort the next action of your rival. You can not only attack your rival but also gain trust from your boss.

<Zongwu's word>When applying the above rule there are different ways, such as, fabricate evidence, run off at the mouth, use fake to make authentic, use one true to make nine false etc. Whatever form, it is false.

145

Rule 54:
Attack crux behind to force rival to surrender
暗击要穴，逼上梁山

《宗吾真言》要想把对方逼入"墙角"，束手就擒，最好的办法就是"釜底抽薪"。在对手实力比较强的时候，不去同敌人正面较量，而是转而破坏敌人所依附的有利条件，瓦解敌人的嚣张气氛。就像一只气球，如果被放了气，自然就飞不起来了。

<Zongwu's word>If you want to force rival to the dead end the best way is 'take a drastic measure to deal with a situation'. When rival is strong you do not fight with him face-to-face, however sabotages all his favor terms to disintegrate his arrogant behavior. After that your rival will like a balloon can not fly anymore due to no air inside.

Code 7:
More talk, more trouble
是非皆因多开口

Rule 55:
Try to make good showing but surround by enemies
意气之争，四面树敌

《宗吾真言》在世上众多"意气之争"中，"口舌之争"是最没有意义的，由此而引发的矛盾也是最不值得的。古往今来，为呈口舌之快，而导致君臣离德、父子离义、夫妻离心的事例不胜枚举。

《宗吾真言》喜欢"口舌之争"人，好像天生就是与别人作对，他们喜欢说的话就是"我就不信..."这种人最大的问题就在于过分"自我"，他什么都要比别人强。

《宗吾真言》喜欢"口舌之争"的人，除了"嫉妒心"过强之外，就是有爱钻牛角尖的性格。他们并非不懂得孰轻孰重，只是这种爱钻牛角尖的性格，限制住自己的思路，最终自觉不自觉地走入死胡同。

<Zongwu's word>In so many spirits' fight, fight in talking around is pointless and worthless. In all ages, there are so many cases about apart from king and official, father and son, husband and wife due to fight in talking around.

147

<Zongwu's word>Someone who likes fight in talking around seems to oppose to others in nature. What they like most is: "I do not believe…" The biggest problem of them is excessive 'egoism' and seems they are better than others.

<Zongwu's word>Someone who likes fight in talking around likes to study insoluble problem besides excessive jealousness. They know the priorities. Their personal traits which like to study insoluble problem will limit their view and finally will go to dead end consciously and unconsciously.

Rule 56: Try to ask sb. do sth which he can't do but finally cause trouble oneself 强人所难，自种祸根

《宗吾真言》古人总结出的处事哲学"忠絮待人，不强人所难"，既是一条避害保身的原则，更是厚黑口才的一条规律。这方面的阐述、名言、警句有很多，都是在认识到强人所难得危害性之后，才总结出来的。

《宗吾真言》为了维护自身利益，向别人提出要求，这本无可厚非，但是如果做事太倔，不给对方一点回旋的余地，最终把对方逼上绝路，自己也会落个"鸡飞弹打"的结局。

<Zongwu's word>The life philosophy from the ancients was: 'be gentle to others and do not try to ask somebody do something which he can't do', it is not only a rule to protect oneself but also a discipline of 'thick black' talks. There are so many statements, wisdoms, proverbs which are summarized from examples of the above rule.

<Zongwu's word>It is natural to ask someone to do something to protect yourself. However, if you do not give leeway to one and force him to dead end, finally you will go to dead end.

148

Rule 57:
Go for wool and come home shorn overreach oneself due to over-clever
机关算尽，弄巧成拙

《宗吾真言》厚黑行世者必须要讲究策略和手腕，如果没有权谋，也不是厚黑行世了。但是一定要看对象，小聪明蒙一蒙糊涂蛋是可以的，但是遇到了"门清"的主就不灵了，否则只能是"偷鸡不成反蚀一把米"。

《宗吾真言》常言道："千穿万船，马屁不穿"。是不是说上司喜欢拍马就可以无所顾忌了？其实，官场上要小聪明欺骗上司同样会引火烧身，不忘"拍马屁拍到马蹄上"的教训。

<Zongwu's word>'Thick black' person must have strategy and tactics. However, one must pay attention to his audience. If one uses petty trick to cheat simpleton, it works. But it does not work for sharp people. Otherwise one will 'go for wool and come home shorn'.

<Zongwu's word>It is said that if one is good at bootlicker, everything is Ok? No, not everyone likes this. One can draws fire against oneself if one uses petty trick to cheat his smart boss.

Rule 58:
Hard to avoid trouble due to frank and outspoken
漫不经心，难免有失

《宗吾真言》要避免因语言上的漫不经心而招致失败，必须把后果的危险性想得严重一些。也就是说，在运用语言时要保持高度的警惕性，时刻记住"是非皆因多开口"，"智者千虑"尚且" 必有一失"，过分自信而掉以轻心，可能就不是一失，而是二失、三失、四失，最终失得一塌糊涂。

《宗吾真言》人生并不是轻轻松松就可以获得胜利的，激烈的竞争和不可逃避的责任，无时无刻不在压迫着你。如果漫不经心，必然当断不断，后果可想而知。

\<Zongwu's word>If one wants to avoid loss from his talk one must pay attention to it seriously. Therefore, keep alert and remember the code 7. If one is over-confidence one will lose finally.

\<Zongwu's word>Life is constantly fight, one can't avoid fierce competition and responsibility. If one does not watch out, one will bear serious consequence.

Rule 59:
Get more kicks than halfpence due to competition
争强好胜，得不偿失

《宗吾真言》曾国潘曾写过这样一首诗："善莫大于絮，德莫大于妒。知足天地宽，贪得宇宙阻"。在宗吾看来，只有自私心重、贪欲极为深的人，才会整天为了争取名利而绞尽脑汁。

《宗吾真言》在人际关系中，当多重矛盾纠结在一起时，假如你并非"系铃人"，那你最好"闭起嘴巴"， 别添乱，在客观环境一时无法改变，条件尚未成熟之时，索性鼓做愚人，静观其变，气定神闲。

\<Zongwu's word>If one has selfish and greed one will cudgel his brain for fame and gain.

\<Zongwu's word>In human relationship, when there are many conflicts, and one is not the key person to solve them, one had better shut up and wait.

Rule 60:
Be unruly to cuase jealous
狂放不羁，遭人嫉恨

《宗吾真言》读书人往往比较聪明，但是如果聪明反被聪明误，说起话来为了让别人知道自己聪明而显示聪明，就犯了大忌。书生气太浓和满脑子"不合时宜"是读书人的通病。

《宗吾真言》有一种人说话从来不顾及别人的感受，非常容易伤人自尊。他只图自己快活，说话刻薄不饶人，这样就会激起巨大的矛盾，甚至会一世为仇。

《宗吾真言》如果你仅仅作一个老白姓可能还好一些，如果身在官场，那么说话方面就要格外小心了。那些能够爬上显位者，为了升官，吹牛拍马，打击对手，送礼进贡，攀亲附贵。在这种弱肉强食的世界里，狂放不羁的下场只能被人"吃掉"。

<Zongwu's word>Most of time scholars are smart, but do not be over smart to flaunt your smart. It is common fault to be bookishness and behind the time for scholars.

<Zongwu's word>Someone never considers other's feeling and often hurts other's dignity. He cares about only himself and talks bitterly and sarcastic. It will cause big conflict even become enemy in lifetime.

<Zongwu's word>If one is ordinary people it is fine. However, if he is official he must talk carefully. How to become successful senior officials? One must flatter, attack rival, bribe and claim kinship. In this competitive environment, 'be unruly' can be got rid of by rivals.

Rule 61:
The more one tries to hide, the more it exposes becuse of self-glorification
自吹自擂，欲盖弥彰

《宗吾真言》在世人眼里，喜欢自吹自擂的人，其装腔作势实际是一种心虚的表现，他们知道自己本来不行，所以才摆出这种姿态，以使自己能够在他人面前有"尊严"和脸面。

《宗吾真言》在与人打交道之中，不注意言语的轻重是一种非常危险的做法。《周易.系辞》上说："君子的话很少"。孔子也把语言作为祸的根子。要想招若是非，没有什么比"自吹自擂"更容易的了。

《宗吾真言》老子曾告诫孔子说，一个聪明而富有洞察力的人身上经常隐藏着危险，那是因为他暴露了别人的缺点。这就是"自是不彰，自夸不长"的道理。

<Zongwu's word>In people view if one who likes glorify oneself will feel guilty for his attitudinized. He knows that he is incompetent and hopes to keep his face and dignity in such behavior.

<Zongwu's word>In building relationship with people one should weigh what one says. Confucian considered talk as a disaster because more talk more trouble.

<Zongwu's word>Laozi lectured Confucian: one who is sharp and observing is dangerous because he unveils other's shortcoming. That's the above rule.

Rule 62:
Extremely arrogance causes despised
夜郎自大，众人不齿

《宗吾真言》在生活中有很多像夜郎国国王那样的人，他们以井底之蛙见看世界之大。有些本事，但由于见识浅薄，胸襟狭窄，以为天下唯我独尊，结果在说话中闹出许多笑话来。

《宗吾真言》"夜郎自大"还有一种表现，就是好为人师。好为人师的人，常常喜欢以高人一等的姿态出现，动则指手画脚，口沫横飞，以为只有自己的见解才最具有指导性。

<Zongwu's word>In real world someone has some skills but narrow-mind, extremely arrogance and extremely conceited, as a result he is despised in talk.

<Zongwu's word>Another behavior of 'extremely arrogance' is: one likes to lecture. He shows his superior and likes to make criticism and thinks that only his opinion is right.

Rule 63:
Lose rationality due to bristle with anger
怒发冲冠，丧失理智

《宗吾真言》在日常生活中，"怒发冲冠"最大的危险性，就是怒而失言，说话没轻没重，冲口儿处，只图一时之快，完全忘记了考虑一下是否该说，结果给自己带来严重的后果。

《宗吾真言》孙子说："主子可怒而兴师，将不可温而致战"。《老子》也说："轻则失跟，躁则失君"。就是说，轻率行动必然失去根基，急躁妄动必然失去主宰。因此，不可轻率从事，不可性情急躁，不可心血来潮。

<Zongwu's word>In real world the most dangerous of
'bristle with anger' is talk in rash. One is quick and
thoughtless in speech and forgets to consider what can be
said and what can't be said and the consequence incurred.
<Zongwu's word>Do not act rashly, be patience and do not
seize by a whim.

Code 8:
Plan in long-term to strive to one's goal
长线方能钓大鱼

Rule 64:
One can't get 'instant success'
急功近利，欲速不达

《宗吾真言》运用"长线方能钓大鱼"的第一禁忌，就是急功近利。也就是说，要达到说服对方合作的目的，不可急躁，这样往往会欲速而不达。

《宗吾真言》为了使对方与自己合作，采用"长线方能钓大鱼"方法，还有一个重要的方面必须关注，就是不能道跑到黑，在正常的情况下不行的时候，最好采用逆向思维，从相反的方向寻求突破。即我们在说服对方合作时，要多开脑筋，强攻不成，逆向突破。

<Zongwu's word>When you apply code 8, the first taboo is 'instant success'. Thus if you are inpatient you can't convince someone to cooperate with you.

<Zongwu's word>When applying code 8 you must pay attention to another important factor: if you can't convince others to cooperate in normal way, you should adopt converse-thinking and seek breakthrough from opposite direction. Therefore when you want to convince others to cooperate you should apply different approaches.

Rule 65:
Step by step to avoid difficulty
由浅入深，避免被动

《宗吾真言》要打动和说服别人，最好是使他自己情缘。同时，还必须认识到，人的需要时各不相同的，各人有各人的偏爱喜好。只要知道了对方的真正意愿，就可以依照他的偏好去对付他了。

《宗吾真言》"由浅入深"的目的就是"避免被动"，这其中，最困难的就是刚开始时，不了解对方的虚实。因此，一定不要过早表露自己的想法，不妨用一种语义模糊的话来进行试探，以便针对性地"由浅入深"进行说服，使对方心甘情愿地与你合作。

<Zongwu's word>If you want to convince and move someone the best way is on his own accord. At the meantime you must recognize that different people have different needs and preferences. Only you know his real intention then you have a suitable solution to handle.

<Zongwu's word>When applying the above rule, the most difficult is at the beginning because you do not know someone's real situation. Therefore never express your idea too early, maybe you can use dark word to test first. After you know his real intention you should have right solution to convince him to cooperate with you willingly.

Rule 66:
Make a small concession to get big reward
将欲取之，必先与之

《宗吾真言》先说出与本意相反或无关的言论，待对方表态后，在巧妙转移，最终使对方同意与你合作的方法，就是"长线方能钓大鱼"中的欲擒故纵之法，它是"将欲取之，必先与之"的直接表现。

《宗吾真言》有没有一些办法使你提出要求时，减少对方回绝的可能性？方法是有的，比如，送礼以堵住对方的嘴巴，拉近双方的距离。毕竟运用物质刺激是"将欲取之，必先与之"本意。

<Zongwu's word>You can talk your unrelated or opposite comment to test someone's reaction, then transfer to your topic to ask him to agree to cooperate with you. That's the above rule.

<Zongwu's word>Is there any solution that when you ask something to reduce the possibility of someone's denial? It is possible, for example, give someone a gift to stop his blabbermouth and get closed relationship. That's the purpose of above rule to use materials to get what you want.

Rule 67:
Seem no purpose but plan actually
看似无意，实则有心

《宗吾真言》"看似无意，实则有心"之法，可以从侧面下手，已话他说，既摆明自己的立场，有助于解决问题，又能顾及自身，让对方明白事情，同时给双方都留了后路。同一句话，借他人说出不尽自然而然，亦可诱导对方开口，无疑是上上之策。

《宗吾真言》既然是通过"看似无意，实则有心"的方式放长线钓大鱼，就不能郑重其事的提出问题和看法。因为这种方式显得过分重视和正式，一旦被否定，会使自己很艰难。

《宗吾真言》还有一招可以达到"看似无意，实则有心"的效果，就是"有理有情"，这样既可以使对方感到理亏，又可以使对方感到形污，最后只好乖乖的采取合作的态度。

\<Zongwu's word>When applying the above rule you can start from other's word. You express not only your opinion and protect yourself but also let someone understand and solve problem helpfully. It is the best strategy to use other's word to lure someone to talk.

\<Zongwu's word>Since applying the above code and rule you can't lodge the question and idea too formally. Because this way seems too formal and serious, if it is denied you will feel embarrassment.

\<Zongwu's word>When you apply the above rule there is another technique such as, 'reason and sentiment' to make someone feel guilty and embarrassment, finally he will cooperate with you.

Rule 68:
Endure to wait for the opportunity
百忍成金，媳妇成婆

《宗吾真言》要达到"长线方能钓大鱼"的目的，一定要善于装"孙子"。自己首先不要小看"孙子"，只有"孙子"才有做"爷"的希望，也才有做"爷"的资格。因此，有做"孙子"的机会一定不要放过，而且"孙子"还要做的有滋有味。

《宗吾真言》"百忍成金，媳妇成婆"，一般只用于对方有才华、能力强、不易对付的人，是没有办法的办法。若对方是个昏庸之辈，根本就不用"熬"，应巧用计谋，将他拿下便是了。

《宗吾真言》说服别人的过程往往不是一帆风顺的、一说即成的。许多人因受不了失败挫折感的折磨，闷闷不乐，长吁短叹，或者哭天抹泪，要死要活，花样百出，这在"厚黑之士"看来太不值得。当然如果是装出来的哪又另当别论了。

<Zongwu's word>When applying above code if you want to get what you want you should pretend to be 'grandkid'. Only you are 'grandkid' then you can be 'granddad'. Therefore if you have a chance to be 'grandkid', just do it and must be happy.

<Zongwu's word>The above rule is using to deal with capable and competent people. If someone is ordinary one you can apply tactics to take down him.

<Zongwu's word>Convincing someone is a long-term process. Most people give up due to confusion and frustration. In 'thick black' person's view, it is worthless. Of course if you pretend that's different.

Rule 69:
Make up-close to force one's cooperation
告于逆势，迫人就范

《宗吾真言》既然劝说别人的过程是一种心理较量过程，在这场较量中最困难的就是相持阶段。这一阶段对方可能提出一大堆里由来搪塞或拒绝。"长线方能钓大鱼"告诉我们，正面强攻不下时，不妨试着换一个角度。

《宗吾真言》如果对方是一个蛮横的人，这时仅动之以情，晓之以理地说服他与你合作就不够了，这些手段只是扶助的，最主要的应找到对手的要害之处，敲山震虎，逼迫其低头。

《宗吾真言》 有些人龟缩躲避、遮掩能力很强，一般情况下很难露出庐山真面目，对于这些深藏不露的人，要使他们乖乖合作，必须巧妙的实施压力，使对方在举措失当的情况下，露出"狐狸"尾巴。

<Zongwu's word>Since convincing others is a psychological contest, the most difficult one is locked in a stalemate. During this process, the counterpart may present different reasons to hesitate or deny. The above code tells us: if you can't attack face-to-face try another solution.

<Zongwu's word>If the counterpart is outrageous, 'reason and sentiment' does not work.
Therefore you should find out critical weakness and attack it to conquer him.

<Zongwu's word>Someone hides deeply, normally you can't see his real situation. Therefore you should put pressure skillfully to unveil his real situation.

Rule 70:
Be insatiable to intimidate one to agree
得寸进尺，如影随形

《宗吾真言》人都有自尊心，特别是中国人更加好面子，对于厚黑行世者来说，这就是弱点。抓住这个弱点，利用使对方"没面子"的行为，胁迫对方答应你的要求。

<Zongwu's word>Everyone has self-esteem especially for Chinese, that's the weakness for 'thick black' person. Crab this weakness and make someone lose his face you can intimidate him to agree to you.

Rule 71:
Go around in circles, then to topic
兜个圈子，再奔主题

《宗吾真言》在说服别人的过程中，有时会遇到这样的情况：有人因为依仗某些势力，说话高高在上，且咄咄逼人，此时，最好的办法就是沉默，这样反而会有助于你的劝说工作。

<Zongwu's word>During convincing others sometime you will encounter such situation: someone shows aggressiveness and arrogance due to his high social status. At such situation the best way is silent to help you to persuade.

Rule 72:
Use both hard and soft tactics
to get what you want
软磨硬泡，金石为开

《宗吾真言》"软磨硬泡，金石为开"在劝说别人合作中有着神奇的魔力。这种方法看来有点不可思议，但是有时只有这样才能达到目的。因为，对方因种种原因拒绝你，而此事又是合情合理，这种情况下只能"磨"了。

《宗吾真言》有时要说服别人与你合作，简直要"跑断腿，磨破嘴"，因此，要运用"软磨硬泡，金石为开"的办法，必须有"铁棒磨成针"的心理准备。

《宗吾真言》"软磨硬泡，金石为开" 这一说服之术，其实质是以消极的形式争取积极的效果，是通过表现自己不达目的决不罢休的决心和毅力，给对方施加压力，以增加接触机会，更充分的表明自己的态度，以影响对方的态度。

161

<Zongwu's word>It is amazing to apply the above rule. It seems incredible but it works. If it is 'reason and sentiment' and the counterpart deny you in different reasons, that's the only way.

<Zongwu's word>Sometime you want to convince others to cooperate with you, you must try every means and solutions. Therefore you should be patient and proactive to apply the above rule.

<Zongwu's word>The technique of the above rule is using negative mean to get positive result in substance. Therefore you must show your determination and perseverance to put pressure to the counterpart to demonstrate your attitude to influence him.

Code 9:
Witticism can get rid of embrassing situation
妙语解开尴尬境

Rule 73:
Mock oneself to get rid of embarassing situation
自嘲自讥，妙口回春

《宗吾真言》在与人交流的过程中，一句话不小心，就有可能引起别人的误解、反感，甚至恼火。在这时候，如果你懂得"自嘲自讥，妙口回春"之法，就可以让对方有火发不出。

《宗吾真言》一些社交场合，可能会遇到了"下不了台"的尴尬局面，这时"自嘲自讥，妙口回春"同样可以发挥作用。你只要懂得如何采取一种有趣的方式来说话，就能很体面的摆脱尴尬。

《宗吾真言》在社交场合，几乎每个人都会不由自主地"吹几句牛"，或说些无关紧要的"谎言"。可是如果当场露了"馅"，处理不好往往是很尴尬难堪的，遇到这种情况该怎么办呢？

事实上，言语交际中，"痴言呆语"会使你的语言幽默风趣，妙趣横生，创造轻松、活泼、诙谐地交际气氛。故作"痴言呆语"会让人感到"荒唐至极"，瞬间思考后便恍然大悟，觉得巧妙绝伦，谐趣无穷，发出会心的微笑。所以，一要扮演呆人角色；二要让人明白你的意思；三要打破 生活常规。

<Zongwu's word>When you communicate with others sometime just your careless one word will cause other's misunderstanding, disguise, even anger. At the moment if you can apply above rule the counterpart will feel embarrass to anger.

<Zongwu's word>In social occasion sometime you will encounter embarrassment situation that you 'can't step down'. At the moment it works to apply above rule. If you can make your talk funny you may get rid of embarrassing situation.

<Zongwu's word>In social occasion sometime people will brag and boast. If it is exposed and if he can't handle adequately it is embarrassed. How? At the moment, you can use humor, funny and mockery talk to create easy and vivid talking environment to ease embarrassment situation.

Rule 74:
Mediate to help one to solve problem
圆场救火，替人解围

《宗吾真言》在人际交往中，少不了矛盾与纠纷。只要有矛盾和纠纷，就免不了劳驾”和事老“来显身手。事实上，只要把”妙语解开尴尬境”用纯熟了，世上没有劝不开的架，没有解不开的死疙瘩。

《宗吾真言》说服力是成为处世赢家不可缺少的要件。大多的纠纷并非一定想动武，一般都是文戏。因此掌握调解纠纷、化解矛盾的语言艺术就会非常有处出了。

《宗吾真言》在社交活动中，能适时地给人面子，给人台阶下，是"圆场救火，替人解围" 的一大原则。然而，台阶怎么给？"场"应该怎么"圆"？火应该怎么"救"？

《宗吾真言》与人交际，很多场合容易让人让己感到难堪，比如指责、批评、拒绝等。这个时候是对一个人为人处世能力的考验，凡在类似的场合擅打圆场者，一般说来肯定会人缘不错，而且还有领导天分。

<Zongwu's word>In social occasion there are arguments and conflicts, therefore it is a good chance for mediator. If you can apply the above code skillfully it is not difficult to mediate them.

<Zongwu's word>Convincing is an indispensable skill for winner. Most conflicts need not assault but only language game. Therefore it is useful to master mediation skill.

<Zongwu's word>In social occasion if you can maintain one's face and find the step for him, it is the big principle of the above rule. However, how to give step, how to mediate?

<Zongwu's word>In most social occasions, denial, criticism and blame will cause embarrassment of others and you. It is time to test your ability to mediate. If you can mediate to help one to solve the problem you have good human relationship.

Rule 75:
Use fun and laugh to make one reflection
嬉笑怒骂，促人自省

《宗吾真言》如果你的上司本身就是一个比较开明的人，很容易就能点醒他。但是，如果他是一个非常刚愎自用，或非常不开窍的人，怎么办？这时不妨先激怒对方，以这种方式出动他的心灵，使其开窍。

《宗吾真言》以激怒对方的方式来说辨，的确存在着一定的危险，那么有没有安全一点的方式呢？可以即兴利用一些由头，运用夸张的形式，制造一些笑料，逗引对方开心，使其在开心之后，又能进行深刻的思索，从而得到启发。

<Zongwu's word>If you boss is open-mind it is easy to convince him. However, if he is
perversity and stubborn, how? At the moment try to provoke him to have his ideas straightened out.

<Zongwu's word>There is risky to provoke someone, any safety solution? Maybe you can use improvisation, or exaggeration to amuse him. After fun he will reflect and be enlightened.

Rule 76: Deliberate confusion to transfer one's attention 故作糊涂，转移注意

《宗吾真言》人言家丑不可外扬，自己的难言之隐谁也不想示人，落下笑柄。善于遮羞不可或缺，一来可以尽量保守秘密，二来丑事曝光后，可以自己避免处于过于尴尬的境地。

《宗吾真言》在遮羞的过程中有时顺势借力也是较为巧妙的方式，因为有丑在先，强行捂住，只能欲盖弥彰。而急中生智顺势借力式的幽默是不会若人反感的。大家笑一笑，便不会再最追究什么了。

《宗吾真言》人最见风节的地方，就是面对名利；人最容易露怯的地方，还是面对名利。所谓志向高尚的人，并非他不要名利，而是看得比较淡而已。

<Zongwu's word>It is said 'no good to spread family scandal' or to speak out painful topic. Therefore you should be skillful at covering up scandal to keep the secret or avoid embarrassing situation.

<Zongwu's word>In covering up your scandal sometime you can take the advantage of an opportunity to turn adversity. Because since it is scandal finally it will be exposed. Therefore you should show resourcefulness in an emergency to take the advantage of opportunity of humor to get favor.

<Zongwu's word>The most care or scare of people is fame and gain. So called noble people with aspiration still need fame and gain without seriously.

Rule 77:
Tit for tat, requite like for like
针锋相对，以牙还牙

《宗吾真言》如果对方蛮横无理，强词夺理，甚至用荒谬的理由攻击你时，最好的办法就是用他们的荒谬逻辑去形成一种理论，反过来去制服对方，也就是 人们常说"以予之矛，攻予之盾"。因为这一类人一般情况下很难正面去说服的。

《宗吾真言》对付总想高人一等、压人一头的人，有时还不妨反唇相讥。这里所说的反唇相讥，既然属于"妙语"， 就必须藏中有露，露中有舱，而不能"真刀真枪"、" 明火执仗"。

<Zongwu's word>If someone is outrageous even uses ridiculous reason to attack you, the best way is to apply above rule to conquer him because it is not easy to convince such person.

<Zongwu's word>If you want to deal someone who is always show his superior and arrogance sometime you can recriminate to persuade him.

Rule 78:
Exaggerate to some extend to get expectation-beyond
意料之外，情理之中

《宗吾真言》要达到"意料之外，情理之中"的效果，必须首先了解它与智慧之间的关系，充分认识到这种说话方式，绝不是单纯的为了幽默而幽默。

167

《宗吾真言》为了表情达意的需要，故意言过其实，对客观的人、事、物作扩大或缩小地描述，通过这种极度夸张，可能喧染出喜剧效果。这可以作为"意料之外，情理之中"的一种表现形式。

运用夸张这一手法，一定要把夸张推向极度。就是把它推出言语的范畴，用情节来表现夸张，这样才能产生戏剧的效果。

<Zongwu's word>If you want to get the desirable result for the above rule you must understand its relationship with wisdom and recognize thoroughly, and this talk way not just for humor.

<Zongwu's word>To express your idea sometime you deliberate to exaggerate people, affair and matter to get comic result. That's the one of ways of above rule.

Rule 79:
Use sweetwords to make joke
花言巧语，制造笑料

《宗吾真言》词语翻覆通常使人感到说话者的愚钝迟滞，把同样的话说了一遍又一遍，必然会若起听着的厌烦。可是，词语翻覆用的巧妙，却可以产生幽默的效果。

《宗吾真言》巧妙的运用一语双关，同样可以达到"妙语解开尴尬境"的幽默效果。比如，谐音双关，利用同音字造成双重意义，体现言在此而意在彼得说话效果。

<Zongwu's word>People will feel boring about 'word smashup'. However, if you can apply skillfully it will come into humor result.

<Zongwu's word>If you can use 'double meaning' word you can get the humor result of the above code.

Rule 80:
Use 'reduction to absurdity' to reason one's flasehood
接过语头，顺势演义

《宗吾真言》对方的意见原来只考虑到一方面的效果，而忽略了另一方面的影响以及可能产生的作用。运用归缪论证，有意朝着这些方面推导，在推导过程中适当夸大，这样就使谬误更加明显。

《宗吾真言》苏轼的《情诗》中云："若言琴上有琴声，放在闸中何不鸣？若言声在指头上，何不于君指上听?" 这首诗就运用了一种诡辩推理，让你明知不对却无懈可击。

<Zongwu's word>Sometime the counterpart only considers one side effect of his opinion and forget another side effect. If you can use 'reduction to absurdity' to reasoning it is obvious to see the falsehood.

<Zongwu's word>Su dongpo used 'reduction to absurdity' to reasoning in his poem. You know he was not right but you can't attack him due to flawless.

Rule 81:
Talk cheerful in irony and jeer to convince one
笑语寓讽，语中带刺

《宗吾真言》讥讽就是一种"笑语寓讽，语中带刺"之术，其运用之妙就在于，带"刺"而不伤人，既达到了反对对方的目的，有不至于引起被讽刺者的恼怒。

《宗吾真言》为了让对方知错，善于运用"笑语寓讽，语中带刺"的人可以采用夸张之法，对所反对之事直指，但顺着对方之意将之加以夸大，最后画龙点睛地指出其危害之处，往往可以收到奇效。让对方明白你话中有话。

《宗吾真言》智激也是"笑语寓讽，语中带刺"的一种重要方法。智激有各种方法：或以激试探对方，或激怒对方引起对自己要说的话的主意，或针锋相对的与他辩论以理服人。

<Zongwu's word>The amazing application of above rule is: no any injury in surface. Therefore you get the purpose to oppose the counterpart but he is not angry.

<Zongwu's word>To let the counterpart know that he is wrong you can apply above rule to exaggerate the matter to make the finishing point finally to get the amazing result and let him know the word beyond.

<Zongwu's word>Another important solution of above rule is: inspire wisely. You can inspire or provoke counterpart to cause his attention or 'tit for tat' to convince him.

www.ingramcontent.com/pod-product-compliance
Lightning Source LLC
Chambersburg PA
CBHW032015170526
45157CB00002B/712